LET'S GET REAL

Our Journey Toward Authenticity and Wholeness

by Dale and Jena Forehand

Published by
Innovo Publishing LLC
www.innovopublishing.com
1-888-546-2111

Providing Full-Service Publishing Services for
Christian Authors, Artists, & Organizations: Hardbacks, Paperbacks,
eBooks, Audiobooks, Music, & Videos

LET'S GET REAL
Copyright © 2010 by Dale and Jena Forehand
Stained Glass Ministries
All rights reserved.

All Scripture quotations, unless otherwise indicated, are taken from the HOLY BIBLE, NEW INTERNATIONAL VERSION®. NIV®. Copyright ©1973, 1978, 1984 by International Bible Society. Used by permission of Zondervan. All rights reserved.

Scripture quotations marked (NASB) are taken from the NEW AMERICAN STANDARD BIBLE®, Copyright © 1960, 1962, 1963, 1968, 1971, 1972, 1973, 1975, 1977, 1995 by The Lockman Foundation. Used by permission.

Scripture quotations marked (NKJV) are taken from the New King James Version. Copyright © 1982 by Thomas Nelson, Inc. Used by permission. All rights reserved.

ISBN 13: 978-1-936076-38-3
ISBN 10: 1-936076-38-1

Cover Design & Interior Layout: Innovo Publishing, LLC

Printed in the United States of America
U.S. Printing History

Second Edition: September 2010

To God,
the restorer of all good things

To our parents,
Jack and Sandra Sadler and Sherman and Gloria Forehand.
Thank you for being our paracletes through the tough times.

To our extended family,
for standing in the gap for us both

To Kelley Cousins-Jones,
for letting yourself be used of God
to help us heal our marriage

To churches,
for opening your hearts and homes
to our ministry

And most of all…

To our children,
Cole and Jorja. You are our heroes
for your courage and comeback
from a devastating experience.

Table of Contents

Introduction 7
Broken Pieces 11
Safe Mates 21
Empty Hearts, Empty Homes 41
A Look at Our Legacy 59
The Shame Train 77
Learning to Love 93
Own Your Stuff 111
Let It Go 125
Making Love 143
Spiritual Wholeness 159
Fragrance of Christ 169
Appendix 175

Introduction

Each of us has a story. Our stories may involve different characters and circumstances, but all have one commonality: they involve a journey. Fortunately, we get to play a part in choosing where the journey ends. The story you are about to read is our journey. It's a story about the death, burial, and resurrection of our marriage. But this story is not just about us; it is about hope—for as long as we have Jesus, we have hope. This is a story about what God can do when He is allowed to invade the lives of people. Our marriage was saved by the pure grace of God. He gave us a broken spirit and a desire to turn from our selfish ways and to completely trust Him in obedience. Out of our willingness to trust and obey, God took us on a journey to authenticity and wholeness. We found that only when we as individuals become whole can our marriage become whole and our house become a home where the Lord reigns.

Perhaps you are reading this book because you have a good marriage but want it to be better. Perhaps your marriage is not what it should be. You may even have a marriage that is struggling to survive. Maybe you are divorced and feel devastated and alone. Whatever your circumstance, we encourage you to walk with us on a road less traveled for *"narrow is the way that leads to life and only a few find it"* (Matthew 7:14).

We have designed this book for individuals who desire to grow in their relationships with Christ, thus strengthening their relationships with their spouse. This book is by no means a quick fix that guarantees your story will have our same ending. That depends on you, your spouse, and your obedience to the Spirit's call on your life. We do guarantee, however, that God's Word is true, that He is faithful, and that He can and desires to do abundantly more than we could ever imagine through His awesome power and grace (1 Timothy 1:14).

Too many times in our lives we have started reading a book with the best of intentions to complete it, but we never make it through. We encourage you to read this book in its entirety so that you can grasp the full intent and hear God's truths throughout. This book should not replace your daily communion with God. It is intended to enhance your walk as an addition to your daily devotion and prayer time.

Begin to prepare your hearts for your time with God as you read the pages that follow. Allow us to offer these suggestions:

- Ask the Holy Spirit to reveal to you areas in your life that need to be crucified. This book is not for you to think about how your spouse needs to hear this! This is a special time of communion with you and God, dealing with you and you alone (Psalm 139:23).
- Ask the Lord to make your heart tender toward His truth and to give you the strength to walk in obedience to His truths. Personal evaluation will allow you to check the condition of your heart as you read our story (John 8:32).
- Ask the Comforter to comfort you as you visit places in your journey so that you can best encourage someone else through your life. As God begins to mold and shape you into His image, you will be able to take your life's experiences and the things the Holy Spirit has taught you as you read and help minister to other sojourners along the way. The fact is, we learn from one another and thus should share with one another what the Holy Spirit has revealed to us (2 Corinthians 1:3–4).

- Ask God to make Himself highly exalted in your life and to draw you nearer to Him. To get the most from this book you must be willing to let God go to the very depths of your soul to do His healing work (James 4:8).

Are you ready to join us on this journey? We are thrilled that God has divinely appointed this time for us. He is ready to meet us wherever we are and to take us, moment by moment, to where He wants us to be. As you read our story, know that God has a story to make of your life and marriage. As He does His awesome work—molding, breaking, and crafting you into His image—don't give up. Stay the course. Our marriages, our families, our friendships and, most importantly, our relationship with Christ will never be the same as we discipline ourselves and yield ourselves to His leadership. Let the journey toward authenticity and wholeness begin!

BROKEN PIECES

"Now to Him who is able to do exceeding abundantly above all that we ask or think or imagine . . ." (Ephesians 3:20)

In 1996, our marriage had reached an all-time low. There was no love, no joy, no relationship. Misplaced priorities and neglect had delivered us to the doorway of divorce. Dale and I (Jena) were both extremely active in church. We had brought two precious children into the world. We had built a lovely house and lived in a favorable part of town. Dale was a new deacon in the church; I was a leading soloist and had just finished writing an Easter musical for the church choir. Together we taught a young marrieds' Sunday school class. From the outside looking in, we seemed to have the perfect marriage, the perfect life. In reality both of us were doing life while neglecting the marriage that had once taken priority.

After years of carelessness, complacency, selfishness, and total disregard for each other, a marriage that had once produced beautiful fruit was now withering on the vine. Suppressed emotional pain developed into a bitter cancer that turned love into hate, freedom into bondage. The wounds we inflicted on each other's hearts left us bleeding to death with no hope for recovery. The pain was so intense that we believed the only way to survive was to get out.

The Marriage Shatters

On a Saturday in July of 1996, Dale walked into our home, took my suitcases from under our bed, and began to pack my clothes. He said that our marriage was over. He told me to get out of his house because he was finished with the relationship. I followed Dale into the bathroom as he packed my things. Dale closed the bathroom door behind me, held it shut, and began to hurl verbal attacks. Our son Cole was banging on the door begging to get inside. When I attempted to leave, Dale held the door strongly and laughed as I struggled to get out.

Dale grabbed our children, Cole (age 5) and Jorja (18 months), and loaded them into his car. As I stood sobbing in the driveway, I could not believe what our marriage had become. Dale sped off with the children and headed for the golf course. Playing golf was a release for him, a way to escape the problems at hand. He had left the children with his mother at the swimming pool. I drove to the pool, gathered the children, and headed to my sister's house to stay for a period of time while things settled. When Dale realized what I had done while he was playing golf, he became incredibly angry. I called Dale and explained that I was afraid of him and wanted to stay away for a while until I felt safe again.

Internal frustrations and lack of control angered Dale. He became so enraged that he began to verbally attack and threaten me. He demanded that I return the children. Thus, I became even more afraid for myself and for Cole and Jorja. After four days, I met Dale at a park so the children could play and visit with him. There was no conversation between the two of us, and the tension was thick.

I did not know that Dale had gone to see a lawyer. The lawyer had made this statement to Dale: "Those kids are just as much yours as they are hers. If I were you, I'd go and get them." For a guy with anger and control problems, this sounded like a great plan.

The next week was Vacation Bible School at our church. I had responsibilities there, so I brought the children and participated as if nothing had happened. While I was cleaning up at the conclusion of the day, Cole was playing in the gymnasium and Jorja was with me at the entrance. Dale drove to the front of the gym determined to get our children. I saw him and quickly ran into the gym to get Cole. As I sat Jorja on the ground and yelled for Cole to come to me, I turned around to see Dale grabbing Jorja and scrambling to the car. Cole jumped into my arms and began asking me what was happening and why his daddy was taking Jorja. Panicked, I repeatedly whispered to Cole that it was all going to be okay. With Cole in my arms, I chased Dale to his car. He drove away.

I then went back into the gymnasium where I met Dale's twin brother Dave. He pulled Cole out of my arms, knocking me to the ground as I fought to hang on to my child. As Dave ran with Cole to the car that waited outside, Cole screamed out for me in hysteria. As I sat on the gym floor, Cole's voiced echoed, "Mommy! Mommy! I want my mommy!" And then there was nothing—nothing but silence.

I sat confused and in shock at what had just taken place. Though people quickly made themselves scarce, a few helped me to my feet and encouraged me to call the police. As my family arrived to help, I began reporting the incident to a policeman who had arrived on the scene. As he wrote the report, he explained that Dale was the father and there was nothing he could do about his taking them. The best advice he could give was to call an attorney.

Meanwhile Dale went to his parents' house, packed some bags, loaded them into his car, and disappeared with the children for seven days. They went to the U.S. Space and Rocket Center in Huntsville, Alabama. They traveled to Chattanooga, Tennessee, to peer through the big glass and see all the fish at the aquarium. For seven days Dale ran from our problems while I lay in a small dark bedroom in my sister's home, destitute, scared, and alone.

After fruitless attempts to locate the children, I picked up the phone and made a call to an attorney, something I had never dreamed of doing. During my first visit, I was advised that the only way to get my children back into the state of Alabama was to file for divorce. The attorney drew up the papers and an officer was sent to serve them to Dale.

On the back roads of a Tennessee highway, Dale's cell phone rang. It was his employer telling him that they had just received papers that read *Forehand versus Forehand*. Dale's heart fell to the depths of his soul as we both realized that we were about to face the most excruciating process we had ever experienced—divorce.

Upon my arrival at the courthouse, I was told that it would be a long process unless Dale and I could negotiate with the aid of our lawyers. We both wanted full custody, however, and both refused to leave the marital residence. That left the judge with no choice but to place us back in the house together pending a divorce trial.

In-House Prison

For 15 months we lived in the house together awaiting the trial date. The house that used to be a home had now become a prison. Dale took the master bedroom and locked me out to find my own place to sleep. I went down the hall and locked myself in Cole's bedroom. I slept with him in his red wrought-iron bunk beds. Many nights I cried myself to sleep while our six-year-old son Cole patted me sweetly on the back.

As time passed, we journeyed back to court on several occasions, each accusing the other of breaking the rules. The judge ruled that we must have the children in the residence by six o'clock every night because of our game-playing, manipulation, and deceit. Being bound to a curfew forced us to spend time together, and our house seemed to get smaller with each passing day.

Because of Dale's anger and desire for control, he withheld all of our money from me. Being a stay-at-home mom, I was reduced to begging from Dale or borrowing from friends and family, a very humbling and shaming experience. Dale would give me a credit card, but one false move and he would rip it away. This push-and-pull between us was evidence that our marriage had completely disintegrated.

We began conducting ourselves as if the other did not exist. We locked doors, separated our clothes and food, and pulled our children from one parent to the other as we each tried to win their love. When we did engage in conversation, our talks escalated into full-fledged arguments that left us wounded and cold. Many fights became so heated that Cole would sit in the corner of the dining room and cry with his hands over his ears begging for it to stop. We threw things, pointed our fingers, and verbally abused each other.

We tried to buy our children's love with gifts. We made plans to keep the other from seeing the children. Manipulation became a learned behavior, and we showed no conscience in the process. The children quickly learned to manipulate as well. There were many situations where they would work the circumstances to force us to be at odds with each other and thus get their own way.

Christmas was a gut-wrenching experience. Splitting time with the children over the holidays was a mess. The lawyers made another trip to the judge because we could not agree on any terms. We could not even agree on a time to go together to get a Christmas tree for the house. So the children and I got one tree and placed it in the den, and Dale took the children and purchased another tree for the dining room.

I had no money to buy gifts for the children, and there was no way that Dale would give me any money to spend on them. I had no hope that I would be able to give my children anything for Christmas. One afternoon a friend called me. She picked me up and took me to Walmart and purchased the children Christmas gifts for me to give them. I stood in the checkout line and cried as the reality of my life began to strike to the core of my being.

Christmas Eve finally came. I came out of the bedroom first and placed my "Santa" gifts out on the den floor. After I went back to my bedroom and locked my door, Dale was then free to come and display his part of "Santa." The next morning was a smothering event as both of us put on our happy faces and pretended to be a family.

Things continued to unravel as two lawyers (who each wanted his client to win) spent time coaching us in the ways of mischief. We paid private investigators. We wore tape recorders to catch the other in some incriminating conversation. We tapped phones and kept perfect records to build our own cases. We provoked the other to anger so we could accuse each other of misconduct. Our house had become a war zone, and the casualties of that war were not only two adults but also two beautiful children.

After we had lived in this hell for 15 months, my lawyer informed me that we would finally get our day in court. The date was set, my lawyer was prepared, and a glimmer of hope that all of this might be over soon was in sight.

The Court Decrees

When our time came up on the docket, I was led into a small courtroom with my lawyer at my side. Dale and I each entered the room carrying a box that represented our lives. As the judge entered and took his place, we rose in honor of his position. The hammer of the gavel meant only one thing: the battle lines were drawn and war was about to be waged.

The next four days were spent listening to family member after family member and friend after friend testify from the witness stand. They had chosen sides, and their goal was to convince the judge what a terrible parent one of us was, thus influencing who should gain custody of our children. Lies and deceit filled the courtroom. Our parents, who once had loved their children's spouses, were now doing all they could to take care of their own flesh and blood. And with every comment came a stab of emotional pain that penetrated to the very depths of our souls. During those four days of trial, it felt as if our lives were being ripped to shreds and placed into our hands. Four days came and went, and as the gavel fell for the last time, we left the courthouse with our arms full of life's broken pieces.

We were told to go back into the house together pending the results of the trial. For the four weeks that followed I felt as if I was smothering, awaiting the outcome that would forever change our lives. At last we received the papers. The divorce was final and joint custody had been awarded.

Hallelujah, it was finally over! Or was it? My depression and anger seemed to be more prevalent than ever before. As my emotions swung from the elation of finality to the frustration of always having to communicate with Dale about matters with the children, I found myself on an emotional roller coaster. Yes, the marriage was over, but life had continued. The struggle for personal agendas, strategic plans, and individual time with the children began to escalate even more. We had to discuss everything pertaining to our children before we could make a decision. And every other weekend, as we passed the children off to the other, we felt as if our own hearts were physically being ripped apart. The anger, frustration, and pain were indescribable.

Divorce. It is a forever funeral as part of us died every other weekend while our children gripped our necks and begged us not to leave. It is what I thought I wanted, and yet I was more miserable than I had ever been before. It affects people physically, emotionally, and spiritually. All that is left is a shattered reflection of what used to be. And the pain associated with divorce cannot be compared to anything except a grievous death.

Stained Glass Marriage

What you have just read is the story of the death of our marriage. Happily, however, the story did not end there. God did not look down from the glory of heaven and say, "Dale and Jena, you have messed things up so badly that I can't fix it anymore." Instead He graciously said, "I'll wipe this clean and help you start over if you will let Me." Two very broken people, not knowing what the other was doing, dragged themselves to the foot of the cross, fell at their Savior's feet, and begged for His forgiveness and help.

One Wednesday morning, four weeks after the final verdict, I called Dale to discuss some gymnastics arrangements for Jorja. Dale, still hanging onto anger from the battle, told me that he would not be taking Jorja anywhere while she was with him, and yet another argument began to brew. Our yelling got so intense that Dale had to close his office door to muffle the sound.

In the middle of this heightened argument, I let Dale see the truth within my heart for just a moment. We call this a window of opportunity. This window occurs when we allow someone to see the purest form of who we are, from the depths of our hearts and without reservations or hidden agendas. The heart is lying out there—exposed, naked, bare. It was the scariest thing I had ever done, but God was pushing me forward to obey His prompting. These words began to flow from my heart in the middle of this downwardly-spiraling conversation: "Dale, what have we done? Why don't you just come get me, and let's fix this thing." Like a bolt of lightning, Dale heard words that shocked him to the core.

Instantly he was faced with a choice. Would he respond with fear, pride, or anger, or would he return my tenderness of heart with the truth of his own? Dale responded with this simple statement: "I can't look at the feet of our children without seeing you." That statement was like a bouquet of roses to me. I didn't think he cared about what I looked like, much less my feet! The Spirit of the Lord began at that very moment to melt the hardened mess of our hearts. The pride, anger, bitterness, resentment, and sheer hatred began to peel back one layer at a time. Within minutes Dale and I were pouring our hearts out while sobbing uncontrollably.

Dale drove to the house where I was staying. He knocked on the door, and a friend of mine who had testified against him in court answered. With great shock and fear on her face, she called for me to come outside. Dale spoke these words from his heart: "Jena, I don't know what all of this means, but I know it is the right thing to do." He kissed me on the cheek and drove away.

We spent the next four months in frequent, intentional marriage counseling with a godly Christian counselor who walked us through the healing process. There were hard days when it seemed like we tap danced on the painful places where we had sworn never to return. Some days seemed like all was fresh and new while others made us question our decision to return to each other. At the end of four months, there was no question in either of our minds that remarriage was what God wanted from us. So on December 21, 1997, we were remarried to the glory of God.

On the morning of our remarriage, Cole entered our bedroom and said, "Since you two are getting together with each other, I think I would like to get together with God." At the foot of our bed, our son prayed with us to receive Jesus as His Savior. Ephesians 3:20 (NKJV) says, *"Now to Him who is able to do exceeding abundantly above all that we ask or think . . . ."* God, in His divine plan, not only brought our marriage back together but redeemed our precious child into His family. His plans truly are greater than we ever could have imagined.

SAFE MATES

"Therefore everyone who hears these words of mine and puts them into practice is like a wise man who built his house on the rock. The rain came down, the streams rose, and the winds blew and beat against that house; yet it did not fall, because it had its foundation on the rock. But everyone who hears these words of mine and does not put them into practice is like a foolish man who built his house on sand. The rain came down, the streams rose, and the winds blew and beat against that house, and it fell with a great crash." When Jesus had finished saying these things, the crowds were amazed at his teaching" (Matthew 7:24-28).

Since you just read our story, you obviously know how broken our marriage was and how awesome our God is! We hope you were encouraged by, as well as reminded of, what God did and still does. He is still a miracle-working God. In a day when couples are choosing to live together instead of getting married and where the impact of divorce is destroying the value of marriage and family, we need to be reminded of a miracle-working God. Just look around you. How are the marriages in your church, your neighborhood, and your sphere of influence doing? Are couples surviving the storms of life? How are the couples you know reacting when the torrent of stress pummels them? Are they handling it like we did—just walking away and allowing their homes to come crashing down? Or are they willing to do whatever it takes to strengthen their homes, protecting them against inevitable storms?

The more we cross paths with couples, the more we are convinced of this one thing: Our problem is not that we don't know what to do; our problem is that we are unwilling to do it! You can hear about the right things to do, but until you put them into practice they are useless! We discovered the hard way that God's ways and God's Word really are the keys to having a successful marriage. But it is so much more than just knowing what God's ways are and knowing what His Word says. It is when we apply His Word and His ways to our daily lives that change really takes place. We do not become proficient in anything without practice, and our marriages are no different.

> You can hear about the right things to do, but until you put them into practice they are useless!

Without question, applying God's Word and ways in our lives has had an eternal impact on us, our marriage, our family and our friendships. We are excited to share with you some of the amazing, transforming truths we have learned in the process of building a house (a marriage) that can stand the test of time. It is our prayer that as you read and practice what you learn, you too will begin the process of allowing God to transform your marriage into a happy, fulfilling, and strong house that can withstand the storms of life.

If we asked you to record the "rains" and "winds" that are currently beating on the house of your marriage, you might write *our financial struggles, our lack of intimacy, our lack of communication, She/He doesn't understand me, She/He is too stubborn.* The list is limitless. So why would we ask that question? Two reasons: one, so that you will be comforted to know that you are not alone—that other marriages are just like yours, with the same struggles; and two, so that after you have applied God's ways and Word to your marriage, you will be able to look back at this question and see what God can do when we partner with Him.

The rock in Jesus' example in Matthew 7 is the applied Word of God. This marriage book or any other marriage resource will be of no value unless the principles taught are practiced within your marriage. Will you commit to apply the truths that you learn as you read this book? We trust that God will strengthen your marriage and enable you to withstand all the "rains" and "winds" that come against you, helping you develop a fulfilling marriage that lasts forever. Let's start by learning how to become safe mates!

Safe Mates

Once God had restored our marriage, we knew there was a ton of work ahead. More than anything we wanted to discover how we ever had arrived at such a broken place. This was absolutely critical since neither of us ever wanted to go back to that place again. What we first uncovered was a slow erosion of connectedness in our first marriage. Over the course of time we had become disconnected due to busyness, neglect, and the demands of life that overshadowed our relationship. We were taking care of our individual roles, pouring our lives into our kids and careers, co-existing in the marriage. Years of this had left us where we just didn't feel "safe" with one another. (When we talk about safety, or becoming safe mates, we are talking about an emotional safety, an intimacy, a transparency where husband and wife can freely (without fear) open their hearts to each other.) We realized that we had lost all emotional safety in our marriage, and fear of the other's response had kept us emotionally severed. Fear in marriage is a huge barrier to being connected. Many couples are afraid to take their hearts out and share them with their spouse. Many are emotionally shut down behind walls of self-protection. They have resolved within themselves that it is safer to keep their hearts close and closed. And when safety is lost, couples find themselves in stagnant, non-emotional relationships.

In 2 Timothy 1:7 we read that God offers us power, love, and a sound mind in place of fear. And in Proverbs 18:10 we read that our ultimate safety is found in the person of Jesus Christ. God used these two scriptural truths to help us push through our fears while striving to regain the safety we had lost. Even in the midst of great uncertainty and fear, we relied on these scriptures and found the power to open up to each other once again through Christ. We relied on the truth that regardless of what happens, regardless of the other's response, our ultimate safety is found first and foremost in the person of Jesus Christ. He is our faithful, good, and loving Counselor, Friend, and so much more. We are safe with Him. Armed with these promises, you too can press through your fears, leaning on His strength to open or re-open your heart so you can find emotional safety in your relationship.

In this chapter we will be looking at the five elements of becoming a safe mate. Each element is based on the person of Jesus Christ, our strong tower of safety. His life will be your guide to reconnecting with your spouse and developing emotional safety in your marriage. As each element is revealed, evaluate how safe you are as a spouse and then ask the Lord to help you take small steps toward practicing these safety truths in your marriage.

Being Available

The first element of being a safe mate is being available. One of the names of Christ is Emmanuel, the "with-us God". He is always available. You don't have to take a number, get in line, or wait your turn. Just as Christ is available to us, we must be available to each other. Unfortunately, way too many couples today are simply too busy to be available to each other. Their marriages are full of separate schedules, tasks to be done, places to go, and lists to check off. The only time they talk is when they have a problem to fix or a schedule to arrange. It happened to us. We were busy doing life, rearing kids, getting things done, and in the process, we lost our connectedness. There were many times when we were in the same room but miles apart emotionally. There is a big difference between being in close proximity and being close in heart.

Some of you understand exactly what we're talking about. You tell your spouse all about your day knowing the entire time that he or she would not be able to repeat a word you had just said. To prove

> **There is a big difference between being in close proximity and being close in heart.**

the point, you could say something like *and then my eyeball fell out* only to hear *Oh, that's good, honey.* Been there? You might as well have been talking to a wall!

I remember one evening when I (Dale) was watching a baseball game. Jena wanted to talk with me but I was way too preoccupied with the game to listen. Now Jena used to have some really stinky feet, so to get my attention she quietly took off one of her shoes and placed it under my nose. Whew, did that get my attention! While this is not the method we recommend, I did realize that without saying a word I had communicated to Jena that the baseball game was more important than she. Since then, I have made it a point to turn off the television and give Jena my full attention when she needs to talk to me. That is what I would want her to do for me, and it communicates that she is more valuable to me than anything this world could offer. Jena has also learned to be patient and gracious by asking if we can talk now or if we need to wait until the game is over. Marriage is a partnership, and it takes both partners growing and learning how to do life together.

Webster defines being available as being present and ready for immediate use; willing to do something. My (Jena) mother had always told me to have the house cleaned, the kids cleaned, and food on the table so Dale could come home to a peaceful place after a long day at work. But sometimes the chaos of life or the unexpected would make our home anything but peaceful! Dale would come in the door and I would be so preoccupied with dinner and schoolwork that I wouldn't even welcome him home or ask about his day. Although I was doing all of those activities for him, I was missing his heart in the process. I learned that if I am going to be available, I have to welcome him into our home with loving arms even if everything is not perfect.

In marriage we may be present but not always ready to receive and serve each other. Being available is more than just being present bodily. It is being ready and willing to do whatever is needed whether it's listening, advising, encouraging, or understanding. It means you are willing to die to your own selfish desires and embrace each other's. You see this in the character of Christ. Revelation 3:20 says that Jesus stands at the door and knocks. He promises that if we will open the door He will come in. Many believe that this Scripture was written for those who need to be saved. The truth is, Revelation 3:20 was written to Christians—those who are already saved! Jesus desires more than salvation for you. Salvation is the doorway for intimacy, community, fellowship, and relationship with Him. He desires more for you than just eternal security from hell. Salvation is the beginning of the journey toward a close relationship with Christ, not the end. In the same way, a marriage doesn't end after you say *I do*; it begins there! Couples who desire an authentic, vibrant marriage must fight to maintain a close, intimate connectedness. Jesus is always available to us. He stands at the door of our hearts ready to join us in intimate relationship. To display His character in our marriages we must do the same. Starting today, begin to make yourself available in your marriage, practicing the very character of our Savior.

Being Approachable

Have you ever been afraid to approach someone? Maybe he doesn't have a welcoming demeanor or his body language or attitude is threatening. Perhaps in the past you've had problems with him so now you just avoid him all together. Or maybe he's snapped at you during previous conversations, leaving you tempted to ask, *Have you seen the piece of my head you just bit off?*

Whatever the circumstances, part of being safe mates with each other is the ability to be approachable.

There have been many times in our marriage when we just didn't feel the freedom to approach each other. We call this the invisible wall. You know it's there. You know something is just not right between you but you dare not approach it. You choose to walk around with this hidden tension and unsettled fear. The warning signs are all around—cold shoulder, short answers, quick comebacks. If unaddressed, this could escalate to complete rejection both physically and emotionally as well as manipulation through the silent treatment, pouting, criticism, and condemnation. When you are continually hurt in your marriage, you begin to condition yourself to become closed, protected, and unapproachable. All of these self-protecting, manipulative, relational responses destroy safety in marriage. Feeling unsafe, insecure, and insignificant in the relationship, an unhealthy couple will try to resolve issues through sex, and for a few days they feel better about their relationship. The problem with this approach is that it masks the real problems and sooner or later they return. More dejected and confused than before, they now find themselves right back in the same emotionally unsafe place and they feel stuck. While it may feel like connectedness, it is only a façade, not authentic.

I (Jena) can remember the fear I felt as I began to put this principle into practice. I was extremely closed since our first marriage had been so hurtful. But as I realized that this was a new and scary place for Dale too, I began to take small steps by faith to allow Dale back into my life, even sharing with him that I was a bit afraid. He was very gracious and confessed that he was scared too, and we slowly but surely began to open our hearts back up to each other.

Consider for a moment the Old Testament duties of the high priest. The old covenant required the high priest to crawl under the veil and offer sacrifices for atonement of the people's sins. Only he was allowed in the Holy of Holies, the most sacred place before God. As the high priest entered under the veil, a rope was tied to his ankle. This was so that if he were struck dead because of his own uncleanliness or failure to complete his duties properly, temple servants could drag him out from under the veil and send in another priest in his stead. Does that sound like an approachable and safe place to you?

When Jesus Christ came as our High Priest and offered Himself as the once-and-for-all sacrifice for our sins, the veil of the temple was rent from top to bottom. We now can boldly approach the throne of grace to receive help in our every time of need. Ephesians 3:12 says, *"In him and through faith in him we may approach God with freedom and confidence."* Now that sounds like safety! We are totally welcome to approach God through Jesus at any time, any place, and with any request. Following Jesus' example of being fully approachable, we too can begin to practice this in our marriages.

When I (Jena) was growing up, there was a man in our church whom we affectionately called Pops because he always had Dum Dum Pops for the children. He knew my favorite flavor was cream soda. Every Sunday I would go looking for Pops because he was warm and welcoming. I knew I could fully approach him. It really wasn't about the sucker he was going to give me; it was more about how loved I felt in his presence. The fact that he could remember my favorite flavor made me feel so special and loved. You see, children are looking for love and acceptance, and they don't run to people who are not safe. Within the marriage relationship, we want to feel as warm, welcomed, and loved in our spouse's presence as I did with Pops—fully loved and fully accepted.

How do we usually welcome children? We bend down and stretch out our arms to welcome them with a big hug. They run into our open arms almost knocking us over with delight while we hold them tightly and lovingly. Mark 9:36–37 describes how Jesus welcomed children with open arms. Mark 15 describes how He welcomes you with open arms—more than 2,000 years ago on a tree at Calvary. His arms are still open today to anyone who will run to Him. He is fully approachable. This is why being a safe mate means that you welcome your spouse with open arms. Safe mates are not fearful about coming to each other and revealing their hearts. Is this true of your relationship? Can you approach each other with anything? If you have not been approachable in the past, maybe it's time to confess and seek forgiveness. As Christ is fully approachable, will you be approachable also? Will you let Christ approach you, and will you approach Christ? Will you be willing to approach your spouse and make yourself more approachable in return?

> **Being a safe mate means that you welcome your spouse with open arms.**

We believe that as you begin to practice approaching God and your spouse as well as becoming a more approachable person, a new depth of connectedness will grow in your marriage relationship. Welcome God and your spouse into conversation and fellowship with outstretched arms. It's a journey less traveled, but one where much love awaits.

Being Accepting

As we grow in safety, we not only need to practice being available and approachable; we also must learn to be accepting of our spouses. There are times when we haven't been accepting of what our husband or wife shares with us. At times, it feels like all our spouse tells us is what we're doing wrong and how much we've hurt him or her. Our first response is to become defensive. *Who does she think she is making such accusations? She needs to control her emotions* or *Stop being so sensitive* or *Just get over it!* Have you ever heard those words? Have you ever said those words? Remarks like these can be definite safety busters. When you are accepting of your spouse in communication, you do three things: you listen, you receive what your spouse has to say in the spirit that it is offered (more on this later), and then you respond with a loving attitude to what you have heard.

When it comes to dealing with others, Ephesians 4:2 commands us to be humble, gentle, and patient, bearing with one another in love. Boy, did we mess this up during the early years of our marriage! How often were we guilty of only partially listening but fully responding. Our defenses were up so high we couldn't even receive or properly evaluate what was shared. We would quickly jump to the defense, especially when we felt we were being blamed. We actually would turn a deaf ear to the rest of what was being said and quickly make a list of everything we could say that would give us leverage or help us win the battle.

Two of the greatest truths we have learned in our marriage are these: First, your spouse is not your enemy. There is no need to jump to the defense, especially without first completely hearing what your spouse is trying to say. Second, you must trust that the heart of your spouse is good towards you. We work really hard to remember both of these. In the midst of our conflicts and misunderstandings, or on those days when we are simply selfish and it is all about us, we remind ourselves, *My spouse is not my enemy and his/her heart toward me is good.* Safe mates accept what their spouses share and even encourage them to speak freely without fear of the other's response.

> **Your spouse is NOT your enemy.**

The power of acceptance in marriage is a wonderful thing. Unfortunately, it is rarely experienced. Many times the very thing that drew us to each other becomes a huge irritation later, and we no longer accept our spouses just as they are. For example, one of the things that endeared Jena to me (Dale) was her outgoing, bubbly, people-loving personality. I loved this about her when we were dating but hated it after we were married. During the early years of our marriage we often got together with friends to play cards or board games or to go to sporting events. That walking, talking, bundle of fun was spending more of her time and attention with our friends than with me! Being the super-sensitive 24-year-old seeking to get some attention, I would make Jena the butt of my jokes in the hope of regaining her attention. I no longer accepted Jena for who she was. This obviously hurt her so Jena would try to tell me how she felt: "Tonight when you made me the butt of your jokes it really hurt my feelings." Again, being the super-sensitive 24-year-old, I would respond with, "Give me a break! It was just a joke! Get over it!" Because I did not accept what Jena had to share, she no longer considered me available, approachable, or accepting of her. If you allow this to go on in your marriage, you will build walls around your hearts and lose emotional safety.

As we grow in our marriage, Jena and I work hard at not interrupting, jumping to conclusions, and getting defensive but rather listening to what the other says and then responding in a loving way even if it means admitting that what we did was wrong. What I (Dale) could have said was, "You know, Babe, I didn't mean to embarrass you. I guess I just wanted to be funny, but that was wrong for me to do it at your expense. I'm sorry. Will you forgive me?" Accepting what your spouse shares and owning the responsibility for your hurtful actions or words promotes growth and healing. Accepting your spouse for who God made him/her to be—even if it is very different from you—offers freedom in marriage. It will strengthen the relationship and develop a connectedness that God will use to draw you closer to each other.

Another common attack on the power of acceptance in a marriage is the desire to change each other. Since so many people marry a person who is their exact opposite, they find themselves in battles over how things are viewed, approached, and resolved. I (Jena) remember counseling a friend of ours with Dale. She talked at length about how her husband doesn't think like she thinks, doesn't act like she acts, doesn't like the same things she likes, doesn't parent the way she parents. On and on the list went until she finally said, "If he would just act, think, and look like me, our marriage would be just fine." Quietly Dale asked her this question: "Dear, is it more important to you that your husband look like you or that he look like Jesus?" As I heard Dale say this, it dawned on me that I had been guilty of the same views. The Holy Spirit brought to mind the many times I had tried to tweak Dale into my image instead of praying that God would transform him into His image. There is power whenever we accept each other where we are but love each other enough not to leave him/her there.

Today I have turned my tweaking into praying. God doesn't need my help to mold Dale into His image, but I get the privilege to pray for him and to then stay out of the way as God does His work. I have also learned to practice verbally expressing and appreciating our differences. After all, it just might be that God brought Dale into my life to reveal some areas in my life that need some tweaking of their own!

> **There is power whenever we accept each other where we are but love each other enough not to leave him/her there.**

God knew that we would need more than His Word but also someone in bodily form who could show us how to put His character into practice. Jesus was the perfect example. Based on John 1:14, Jesus came to earth full of grace and truth. He did not present only truth as that would make us feel as if we could never measure up. He did not offer only grace, tempting us to live like we want because He would always forgive. Jesus came with both grace and truth. He presents truth to us *and* He extends grace and forgiveness as we strive to be like Him. The life of Christ is a clear example of how He made Himself available and approachable to people. He accepted others with great love. He let people know that they didn't have to get it all together, to be perfect, to be in relationship with Him. He loved people exactly the way they were, and He gracefully and lovingly led them to change. If you are going to live as a safe mate, then display the power of acceptance in your marriage by following Christ's example. Accept your spouse where he or she is, and in love encourage your spouse to grow more Christ-like.

Being Accountable

Accountability in marriage can be really difficult. It certainly can be mishandled. One way is when couples use it as a platform to become judge and jury over each other's lives. Author John Eldredge once stated that accountability has been reduced to being each other's "parole officer". We don't need "parole officers" in our marriages; we need partnership.

Another way accountability is mishandled is when it causes a person to walk in perfectionism for fear of disappointing the other. Many fear the potential rejection they would receive if they were fully known. In response, they hide. They hide their concerns, their true selves, and the past baggage they brought into the relation-ship. The continued choice to hide will cause authenticity and wholeness to become strained because accountability is limited to the extent that you allow others into your life. Clearly our fear of rejection, accusation, and condemnation (to name a few) can be very motivating. When this fear is combined with an unhealthy dependency on the approval of others, there is an incredible motivation to keep our true selves hidden. Some people's hearts are so full of pride they will never let anyone see their real selves. They will never admit they have faults or needs. They make excuses and justify their behavior because that is easier than looking deep within and making changes. If a marriage consists of judgment and condemnation, fear and performance, pride and justification, odds are that the safety in that marriage is eroding.

The great news today is this: when true, healthy, God-honoring accountability takes place, the rewards are amazing. Perhaps the greatest reward is that you no longer have to journey to Christlikeness alone. Never forget: God did not create you to go through life alone. You were made in the image of a relational God (Genesis 1:27) who created you as a relational person. We need each other to help us along the way. This is why

> **Accountability is limited to the extent that you allow others into your life.**

becoming safe mates and pursuing authenticity and wholeness is critical for your marriage. Without it we will remain the same and never attain the goal of looking like Christ. That's why we have looked at the life of Christ to find these principles of safety. Also note that they work in order. In other words, before we ever get to the level of healthy accountability in marriage, we must consistently live out the three previous principles (being available, approachable, and accepting). After all, it is hard to make withdrawals from each other without first making deposits. Without mutual deposits, we leave each other emotionally bankrupt. But as we consistently demonstrate the first three principles, we will feel safe enough to open ourselves up for healthy accountability because our hearts are being handled well.

Healthy accountability is not easy. If you really want this for your marriage, you must always keep in front of you the critical elements of honesty, humility, ownership, and partnership. Each of these plays a vital part in creating the environment where you can mutually grow. According to John 8:32, without honesty, it will be hard to know where and how to help each other. Based on Matthew 7:3, without humility spouses can easily focus on the speck in their partner's eye while disregarding the beam in their own. Galatians 6:5 reminds us that without ownership, a spouse will tend to become the victim and not carry his/her own load. And Ecclesiastes 4:9-12 tell us that without partnership, we will become isolated, and isolation destroys intimacy.

Let's say Jena has gone to the doctor because she is having some voice problems. The doctor encourages her to drink a lot of water and to stay away from her favorite drink, Dr. Pepper. After the doctor's appointment, she comes home and shares with me (Dale) what the doctor advised. If I am unavailable, unapproachable, and unaccepting of her and her problem, we are definitely headed for a loss of heart in our relationship. Instead of receiving her, I minimize the doctor's advice and make her feel stupid for even talking to me about it by scolding her for interrupting my baseball game. Realizing that I have screwed up royally, I decide the way to fix this is to take her to dinner. We don't speak all the way to the restaurant. Our waitress arrives, happy and ready to take our drink order to which Jena replies, "I will have the biggest honkin' Dr. Pepper you've got!" To which, I reply: "Oh, no, she interrupted my baseball game for this; she'll have water!"

You see, unless I demonstrate the first three principles of being safe with Jena, I have no business holding her accountable. Accountability without safety will result in resentment and resistance. You can bet Jena will be resentful of my telling her what to do and resistant to my help in the future. But if I have been available to listen to her, approachable by turning to her and receiving her, and accepting of all that she had to say about the doctor, then I can respond to her at the restaurant: "Hey, Babe, don't you think you might drink water? The doctor said it would be better for you," and she would respond much differently. This is holding her heart well. This is how you avoid damaged feelings, promote growth, and strengthen your relationship.

> **Accountability without safety will result in resentment and resistance.**

In a safe marriage, gentle accountability can yield the peaceful fruit of righteousness, offering healing to all who embrace it (Hebrews 12:11–13). Jesus was the perfect example of healthy accountability. As we said earlier, John 1:14 says that Jesus came with both grace and truth. Not only does Jesus hold us accountable by His Word, but He also gives us everything we need to live up to it. He not only speaks the hard truths to us, but He also gives us His Spirit to help us live it out. May your marriage be found full of grace and truth.

Being Vulnerable

As we wrap up this chapter, we encourage you to take some time for reflection and personal application. We truly want you to be doers of the Word and not hearers only. We want you to apply the Word, live the Word, and model the Word. Think about all the messages you have ever heard or all of the lessons you have taught or studied. How many of them really impacted you for life change? If you answered very few, then you also have to ask why. We can't blame the Word of God because we know the Word of God does not return empty, but accomplishes the purposes for which it is sent (Isaiah 55:11). Again, perhaps the problem is not that we don't know what to do; we just choose not to do it. Revelation of truth is God's part; obedience is ours. Hebrews 4:2 says the Word of God had no value to those that heard it because they did not combine it with their faith.

We began this chapter with the principles of safety because unless a couple can move back towards each other and re-connect, they will have a difficult time growing together through the chapters that follow. Developing safety in your marriage can start now by taking small steps towards demonstrating Christ in your marriage. It is only after the previous four elements of safety have been firmly established that the last quality will be exemplified without any hidden agendas or personal reservations.

Our final element of safety is the word "vulnerable". True vulnerability in marriage is when a husband and wife can deeply reveal themselves, legitimately desiring but never demanding a loving response. It's the "no strings attached" principle of being a safe mate. Unfortunately in marriage there is a lot of manipulation, a lot of hidden agendas. There are strings attached to several of our choices, behaviors, and conversations. We say things and do things in order to get things. This is not vulnerability; it is manipulation, and manipulation is a safety buster.

In the early years of our marriage, I (Dale) would do certain things to get my way. I might work around the house because I wanted to go play golf. Or I might say certain things or buy certain gifts because I wanted sex. Sex (physical connectedness) is often the way men get emotionally connected to their wives. It is a step towards their being vulnerable. Women, on the other hand, would define vulnerability as an emotional connection that leads to the physical. Dr. Kevin Leman got it right when he said, "Sex erases problems for men, but problems erase sex for women." No wonder true vulnerability is so hard in marriage! We want the same things, intimacy and connectedness, but we go about obtaining them in completely different ways. Sometimes men need to have sex so that they can talk intimately, and sometimes women need to talk intimately so that they can be comfortable having sex. It's a give and take, and the safer you are with each other, the smoother this goes.

As good and vital as sex is to a marriage, sex is not intimacy and vulnerability. If sex was intimacy, then the United States of America would be the most intimate nation in the world! It's not! Intimacy is simply, "Into me, I will let you see." Sex is not to replace intimacy but rather a road to it for men and a response to it for women. True vulnerability is the opening up of your heart to another, revealing your hopes, your dreams, your feelings, your passions, your failures, and your struggles.

> **Intimacy is simply "Into me, I will let you see."**

Jesus was vulnerable with His disciples in John 15:15 when He said, *"I no longer call you servants, because a servant does not know his master's business. Instead, I have called you friends, for everything that I learned from my Father I have made known to you."* Everything the Father told Jesus, He disclosed to His disciples. Into Him they completely saw. He deeply revealed Himself, legitimately desiring but never demanding a loving response. Jesus was the epitome of being vulnerable.

Now we know that some of you are thinking this all sounds scary, mushy, gushy, warm, and fuzzy. But before you write it off as undesirable and impossible, hear us out. We had such an "ah-ha" moment in our last counseling session before we remarried. Our counselor asked us to sit knee-to-knee and confess how we had contributed to the breakdown of our marriage. Here's what happened, and here's where the five elements of being a safe mate was birthed.

As we sat there, face-to-face and knee-to-knee, Jena began to cry. She dropped her head and couldn't look at me (Dale). Our counselor got out of her seat, knelt beside Jena's chair, and gently lifted her head. It reminds me that God is the Lifter of our heads (Psalm 3:3). She tenderly asked, "Jena, what are you afraid of?" She replied, "Over the course of our marriage, I have repeatedly taken my heart out and placed it in Dale's hands only to have him squeeze the life out of it. I am so afraid to place my heart back in his hands again, because I don't think I can survive another squeeze!" As I (Dale) heard these words, it hit me in the core of my being. For the first time in our marriage, I had come face-to-face with the fact that I was not a safe mate to Jena. Broken, I got on my knees crying and replied, "Jena, if you will give me one more chance, I commit to try, with God's help, to never squeeze your heart again." This openness, vulnerability, and authentic intimacy broke down the walls we'd built around our hearts. We both committed that day to take our hearts out once again, give each other another chance, and really go hard after the principles of safety.

We wish we could tell you that we've never messed up, but to do so would be a lie. We are imperfect people, and there is no such thing as a perfect marriage. We just worship a perfect Savior who daily provides His grace, mercy, strength, and love to help us. On those days that we don't do so well, we are certainly thankful for the forgiveness we receive and are commanded to give. Our firsthand experience can assure you that God will honor your efforts and obedience. We are living examples that even though emotional safety might be lost in your marriage, you can find it once again by becoming a safe mate. We hope you see by now that the five principles of safety, based on the character of Jesus Christ, build upon one another. These building blocks provide the means to maintain a safe environment for a growing relationship. As you make yourself available and approachable, you begin to receive healthy communication from your spouse. As you positively accept one another, you can move into accountability and vulnerability. As you begin to see the development of openness, you are empowered to become more available and approachable. And the building continues.

If you have realized a lack of emotional safety in your marriage, there is hope for you. Perhaps you need to acknowledge where you have not been a safe mate and have not held your spouse's heart well. Do you need a fresh start or a second chance? Then why not ask for forgiveness and let today be the first day of rebuilding safety in your relationship? Authentic safety and intimacy is certainly attainable if you will begin to model the Word of God in your marriage. Christ showed us safety in its purest and perfect form. He was safe then, and is still safe today. He is always available. He is always approachable. He is wholly accepting of us. He holds us accountable by His Word and the convicting power of the Holy Spirit. And He was vulnerable all the way to the cross.

We hope that each characteristic of safety has enlightened you to truth and you have begun to put these truths into practice. Being safe mates is not always easy. A great marriage comes only with great work. Sometimes it feels like it would be easier to let things go and play your roles well, but you will lose connectedness. None of us really want that for our marriages. We must press in to display the character of Christ to one another. Galatians 6:9 says, *"Let us not become weary in doing good, for at the proper time we will reap a harvest if we do not give up."* Isaiah 40:29 says, *"He gives strength to the weary and increases the power of the weak."* Let these be an encouragement to your soul. Stay the course. Your marriage matters. It is important. And if you will cooperate with God and begin practicing these truths, He is going to do some amazing things in your life and marriage.

> **A great marriage comes only with great work.**

Friend, we have purposely designated this initial chapter to help you understand safety and the safe tower character of Christ. This is the foundation upon which we now build. The depth of growth that can result for you as an individual and for your relationship with each other is contingent upon the safety found in an intimate personal relationship with Christ. Out of the overflow of that relationship, God, by His divine wisdom and power, will enable you to become a safe mate. If you have never accepted Christ as your Lord and Savior, we invite you to go to the Appendix at the end of this book and find out how you can experience safety and intimacy with Jesus. Our prayer is that through the remaining chapters, you will accept the challenge to practice safety. Christ is the safest person there is. His name is our safe tower into which we run. So run to His safe tower and then take that safety into your marriage. You will experience a deeper walk with God, and your relationship with your spouse will thrive. Both can become a beautiful testimony of the goodness and grace of our Lord. Hang in there! We still have much to discover on our journey toward authenticity and wholeness.

EMPTY HEARTS, EMPTY HOMES

"But my God will supply all your needs according to His great riches through Christ Jesus, our Lord" (Philippians 4:19).

In the movie *Fireproof*, John, Caleb Holt's father, tells him something profound: "You can't love her . . . because you can't give her what you don't have." What an amazingly true statement! Many couples are so wrapped up in their individual neediness, loving from a deficit and manipulating through wrong motives, that they are living with empy hearts in empty homes. We experienced this firsthand in our own marriage and have witnessed it in the lives of other couples as well. For example, we met a couple not too long ago who had only been married two weeks. They were "goo-gooing" at each other continually. "Pumpkin" was their pet name for each other and they used it liberally. They believed they had the perfect marriage and that the world was a wonderful place because of all the happiness they felt. They had big aspirations for their future together, and life was grand.

Consider Adam and Eve. Theirs was the ultimate, utopian honeymoon in the Garden of Eden. They had the perfect marriage in the perfect place. Adam was the king and Eve was his queen. They were complete, content, and happy. We call this flawless scenario "marital bliss".

Marital Bliss

We all want it. We dreamed of it before marriage, and thought we would achieve it when we married our spouse. The problem was, and remains today, that we've never known what marital bliss really looks like or how to get it. We've tried a myriad of methods only to come up empty-handed. But

> We've never known what marital bliss really looks like or how to get it.

the Word of God has help for us. Through a study of the book of Genesis we have identified three benchmarks of marital bliss: perfection, priority, and partnership.

Perfection. As we began reading in Genesis 2, we found that the Garden of Eden was a place of perfection. This garden had anything and everything Adam and Eve needed. Their physical needs were completely satisfied. Their emotional needs were completely fulfilled. And God was the supplier of it all. They were even in perfect relationship with their Heavenly Father (the Creator) as He walked with them in the cool of the day. It was a perfect marriage, in perfect bliss, in a perfect place.

Do any of us know any perfect marriages today? No! There are no perfect marriages. But does that mean that we are not to strive for perfection? Just as Paul says in Romans 6:1–2, do we continue in sin because of the abundance of grace freely given? The answer to both is *God forbid!* We must be ever striving for perfection in our marriages. We will not reach perfection until our glorification, but until then we must press on toward that goal (Philippians 3:14). If you strive for perfection, you might obtain excellence along the way.

We don't have to be perfect people in order to attain a perfect marriage for the truth is, there are no such people nor such marriages. But rather the perfect Savior, Jesus Christ, compels us and supernaturally transforms us into His workmanship, a masterpiece, a work-in-progress toward perfection. When a marriage is grounded on the perfect life of Christ, excellence in marriage can be achieved. And this is a goal worth striving for. Is your home, your relationship, ever striving for perfection? Is it grounded on Christ and Christ alone? This is the starting point for marital bliss.

Priority. Secondly, the marriage of Adam and Eve held a place of priority. Genesis 2:24 provides the marriage principle of "leave and cleave". The word cleave comes from the Hebrew word *dabag* which means to impinge, cling, or adhere to. It's like taking two pieces of wood, bonding them together with wood glue, and then further attaching them with wood screws for good measure. They are so connected that to separate them would literally destroy both pieces.

This is why God says He hates divorce (Malachi 2:16). He knows that the covenant marriage He ordained for a man and wife is one that so binds them together that separating the two will damage them both greatly. This is why Dale dropped to 145 pounds and Jena weighed only 97 pounds by the end of the divorce. As we separated in heart, we were destroying ourselves from the inside out. God created the marriage relationship to be a priority. The harsh reality is that many times we make our extended family, our children, our friends, our jobs, and even our church the priority of our lives. God created the marriage between a man and a woman as the first and foremost relational priority in our lives (other than our relationship to Him). When we begin to view our marriages as a priority, we are honoring God's design for marriage since the day He ordained it.

> **God created the marriage relationship to be a priority.**

Partnership. Finally, the marriage of Adam and Eve formed a marriage partnership. They were undivided, united in spirit, soul, and body. In partnership you find two people who share something that includes both the triumphs and the troubles. Genesis 2:24 puts it this way: they will become "one flesh".

From the beginning of time when God created the heavens and the earth, He declared all was "good". However, after creating Adam, something was still missing. God said that it was "not good for the man to be alone" for there was no suitable "help-mate" for him (Genesis 2:18). So God created Eve. They were to be partners in life. In partnership we understand that what we do, we do together. Whether you have a golf partner, tennis partner, business partner, or Bible study partner, you are working together for one common goal, embracing both the good and the bad. The same is true in marriage.

In fact, it is more critical in marriage than in any other relationship in life. Yet many times we find ourselves treating our golf partner, tennis partner, business partner, or Bible study partner better than we treat our own spouse! Partnership in marriage means that you and your spouse join hand in hand on your specifically ordained journey with God. Any decision you make needs to be made together. All decisions are for the benefit of the marriage partnership, not your own selfish wants and desires.

> **Partnership in marriage means that you and your spouse join hand in hand on your specifically ordained journey with God.**

Ultimately partnership in marriage includes spending time in prayer, seeking the face of God, and asking Him to lead your marriage (Philippians 4:6). According to John 14:16-17, God has given us the Holy Spirit to help us make our marriages perfect, prioritized, and a good partnership. So the question becomes, *How important is it for you and your spouse to pray, inviting the Holy Spirit into your marriage?* When a marriage is founded on the perfect life of Christ, both husband and wife make each other a priority. They demonstrate genuine partnership and wrap their lives in prayer. That marriage will experience marital bliss by God's design.

Marital Bust

Six months after we met the couple mentioned in the opening of this chapter, we met again. They were sitting in a newlywed couples' Sunday School class with several other couples. When asked how married life was going, the wife quickly responded, "This is not at all what I bargained for!" Not surprisingly, between two weeks and six months, they were no longer experiencing bliss in their marriage. Ever been there—where thoughts of a blissful marriage were replaced by lost hopes and unfulfilled dreams?

Let's look again at Adam and Eve. Because of the craftiness and deceit of the serpent, there was suddenly no more marital bliss for this couple either. What in the world happened in this short period of time to these two couples? What caused marital bust?

From Genesis 2 and 3, we identified three benchmarks of marital bust that were at the heart of our divorce and are instrumental to the breakdown of marriages all over the world. They are shame, blame, and pain.

No one intends to experience marital bust. We surely didn't. And yet it happened. However, if we can identify the destructive forces, we can stand guard for our marriages. Scripture clearly indicates that sin entered the world through the disobedience of Adam and Eve. When sin and disobedience enter a relationship, marital bust is inevitable.

> **When sin and disobedience enter a relationship, marital bust is inevitable.**

Shame. Sin and disobedience many times turn our homes into places of shame. The sin of Adam and Eve greatly affected their relationship with God and each other. They became so ashamed of their sin that they sewed fig leaves together and covered their nakedness. Nakedness was the only thing they discovered through their newfound wisdom. So many times we make choices only to find out in the end that it was simply a poor decision that didn't turn out at all the way we had intended. Adam and Eve wanted to be wise, akin to God. Instead, they felt shame.

When we sin, God, through His Holy Spirit, brings conviction into our hearts. Conviction says, "My behavior was wrong." Satan, on the other hand, attempts to flood our hearts with shame. Shame says, "There is something wrong with me." It implies that everybody else is okay, and everybody else is perfect and can do the right things, but I cannot because there is something wrong with me. I am defective while everyone else is whole. When we allow Satan to shame us, we begin to shame others around us to lessen our "singled out" feelings. We begin to shame others with our words to make us feel better about ourselves. This is extremely detrimental to the marriage because it results in two people locked up in tremendous bindings of the enemy. Words such as "you always " and "you never" are at the core of shaming. Shame keeps people so bound in their wrongness that they cannot fulfill the purposes for which God created them. And if shaming isn't making us feel better about ourselves in a situation, we resort to the next tactic—blame.

> **Shame keeps people so bound in their wrongness that they cannot fulfill the purposes for which God created them.**

Blame. The marriage relationship between Adam and Eve developed into a place of blame. They began to blame each other and God for their own sin. Notice this is the first time we see the age-old strategy of "passing the buck".

Passing the buck started with the first marriage in the Garden of Eden. Today we practice it to avoid personal responsibility in relationships. Adam blamed Eve, and he blamed God. Have you ever blamed God for your situation when it was your own disobedience that got you into trouble? Eve blamed the serpent. We do the same thing. Look at these blaming phrases:

- "Well, I wouldn't have done what I did if you hadn't done what you did!"
- "You made me treat you like that!"
- "I was just reacting to what you said!"

The truth is, we choose each day how we will respond, whether through blaming others or taking responsibility for our own sin. And that is a choice that only we as individuals can make. Nobody can make you do anything. Your behavior is a result of your choice alone. And if ungodly behavior goes unchecked, you can bet you are headed for marital bust.

Pain. If shaming and blaming are common in a marriage, the result is a lot of pain. There were consequences for Adam and Eve's sin that would last a lifetime, and they certainly involved pain. When we sin, we experience the consequences of our actions, and it is usually painful. One truth about sin is that it will take you farther than you ever intended to go and keep you longer than you ever intended to stay. The pain we feel from sin reminds us of our need for Christ. Yet for many, it only makes them cynical and bitter.

If you've ever experienced a cut then you've experienced pain. Over time a scar forms and you are okay. But if you have ever experienced a cut that continues to be re-opened and is never given appropriate time to heal, then you truly understand chronic pain.

During our first marriage and divorce, we used cutting words that went deep, marring the other person. Some of those words left scars that

> **The recurring inflicting of pain damages the soul.**

don't hurt as much anymore but are still reminders of where we've been. Still others left deep wounds on our hearts because they were re-opened time and time again as the shaming and blaming continued. The recurring inflicting of pain damages the soul. Only the miraculous grace of God can repair that damage.

According to Isaiah 59:2, sin affects our relationship with God because it separates us from Him. Once sin entered the garden with all its blame, shame, and pain, it separated man from God. Adam and Eve suffered great consequences for their sin, but the ultimate consequence was the void left in their hearts when they were separated from their Heavenly Father. And though Adam and Eve desperately desired to be back in close fellowship with God, there was a vast chasm between them that would require a bridge over which they could cross. God provided that bridge through His Son Jesus Christ.

Why Am I So Needy?

Just as Adam and Eve were separated from God, we too have allowed sin to separate us from God, the One who completely fills us and gives us purpose and meaning in life. That separation leaves us feeling very empty, like something is profoundly missing. As we desperately try to find a means to fill this void, we often find ourselves feeling needy. We long to be complete, whole, and in perfect relationship with another. That longing was originally meant to be satisfied by God Himself, but because of our separation from Him due to sin, we now search for it elsewhere. We are in need. And though needs are normal, they come with an intense desire that must be satisfied. Many times we do whatever it takes to have our needs met because we hunger so deeply for their fulfillment.

All of us are aware that we have needs. These needs are legitimate, but we are not always wise in our choices of who or what should meet them. The first year of our marriage, we began to notice how much we needed each other to make us feel complete and whole. Frustration and bitterness grew within our home as we tried so desperately to get the other to fill the insatiable void within our hearts.

> **We are not always wise in our choices of who or what should meet our needs.**

I (Jena) came into the marriage with a real need to hear the words "I love you" and "You are so pretty." I didn't understand why, but those words of affirmation were a deep need in my life. I desired to be unconditionally loved, accepted, and trusted. Dale was so young and oblivious to my needs that when I asked him why he never said those things he answered, "When I cease to love you, and when I cease to think you are pretty, I'll let you know." That did nothing except discourage me and drive me further into my quest for fulfillment.

Eve's Curse

Because of sin, Eve was left with a quest to fill her neediness. This quest was formed right out of the curse of her sin, and mothers completely understand her curse. Genesis 3:16 shares with us the curse of pain in childbirth. Many mothers have experienced this pain, so identifying firsthand is not a problem! It is the last part of this verse, however, that we tend to miss, skip, or not understand. As we began to study the latter part of the curse, the Spirit gave us understanding and insight that revolutionized our lives and our marriage.

The last part of that verse says, "Your desire will be for your husband, and he will rule over you." The word desire comes from the Hebrew word *tshuwqah* (tesh-oo-kaw), which means a deep longing for, a craving, a stretching out after, of beast to devour. When sin entered the world, Eve no longer knew the safe, secure, and intimate relationship with God. She was left with a void that longed to be filled. Eve now had a natural tendency to crave, stretch, and even devour Adam to get her needs met. When he could not fully do so to her satisfaction, she tried to rule over him. We call this nagging. As she would demand that her needs be met, incapable Adam would fail to meet those needs, and she would become more disappointed and demanding.

As with Eve, women have a deep longing that needs to be filled. The greatest need in a woman's life is to develop deep intimacy. She wants to feel safe and secure in her relationships. She wants to know that she is deeply loved and that nothing she does, nothing she is or is not, will change that love. She also wants to be

> **A woman's greatest need is to develop deep intimacy.**

confident in the commitment of the one with whom she has a relationship. She wants to know that no matter what happens, her husband is committed. While the need for deep intimacy and security is not exclusive to women, it is the primary need of most women.

In modern culture, when a woman begins to make demands, she is considered a nag. In reality she is behaving within the curse of Eve with her unquenchable longing and stretching out for intimacy. The truth is, there is no earthly relationship that can fully meet that need.

God hand carved the void in your life so you would see your need for Him. Then He sent Jesus to completely fill the void. If someone or something else could fill that void, then Jesus' death as our Savior would have been in vain. And when we look to other people or things to fulfill us, we make

> **God hand carved the void in your life so you would see your need for Him.**

a mockery of Jesus Christ and His death on the cross. We also elevate someone else to a position that belongs to Jesus, and this is idolatry. Christ will share His glory with no one.

Jesus Christ is the only One who can fully meet your need. And yet, spouses, that does not get you off the hook. For every curse there is a calling. Men, now that you know your wife's deepest need for intimacy, safety, and security, you possess the wonderful privilege of pointing her to the very One who can fulfill that need. By doing so, you enhance freedom in the life of your wife. You free her from demanding what she needs from you or others. You free her from being disappointed when nothing else satisfies. You also free yourself from living a defeated lifestyle. All those times when you did your very best to meet your wife's needs and it was never good enough are past. You never have to feel like a failure again. What an awesome calling for men to lead their wives to the unconditional love of Jesus Christ.

In Romans 8:38–39, Paul reminds us that absolutely nothing can separate us from God's love. Nothing you will ever do will make Him love you less. Nothing. God has loved you with an everlasting love (Jeremiah 31:3). It never ends and never goes away. And with that everlasting love comes the promise that we who were once far away have now been brought near (Ephesians 2:13).

Through His Son Jesus, God wants to fill the void that sin left. Jesus' death paid the penalty for your sin and mine, and His blood covered our sins so that we could again be brought near to God, and our needs could again be totally filled by Him. His commitment proved true all the way to the cross. He can be trusted. His love is so unconditional that nothing you do or don't do will change His love for you. He loves the very best of you and the very worst. He loves you, flaws and all. And He wants to fill you to overflowing with His love so that it pours off of you and onto a world that so desperately needs to see and feel it. How it must break the heart of God to offer His only beloved Son to meet our deepest needs and then to watch us shun this incredible gift while searching for what we think is better.

Will you allow God to fill every crevice of your heart with His love and commitment to you? This decision will totally and radically change your life and marriage.

Adam's Curse

Adam was also cursed for his sin. His curse involved the sweating and toiling of work (Genesis 3: 17–19). And with that curse came a root need that is evident in every man.

Meet Jake. Jake had worked for months building a deck for his home. He wasn't building the deck because he was dying to do so. He was building this deck for his family to enjoy. We have heard countless men make this statement: "Everything I do,

I do for my family, and sometimes I feel it's never good enough!" Jake had visions of late afternoon cookouts with friends and family. From this deck he would be able to watch his children play in the yard. He could sit in the morning shade drinking coffee and visiting with his wife. No, this wasn't just a deck; it was a monument of Jake's dedication to his family and his internal sense of accomplishment.

The day of unveiling was finally here. Jake had finished his deck right on schedule for a Labor Day cookout. They had invited friends and family over and had put scrumptious food on the grill. It was going to be a wonderful day. As everyone started to arrive, Jake proudly escorted them to the deck. The compliments were overwhelming yet something was missing. As the others raved about the new deck, Jake realized his wife remained silent. While others lavished him with accolades, he never received approval or affirmation from the one from whom he wanted it most—his wife. It was as if she didn't even care.

At the end of the day Jake sat down to share his hurt feelings with his wife Tammy and said, "Everyone was happy for me and made me feel special . . . everyone but you. You could care less about what I do for you or this family. Does anything I do for you really matter?"

The depth of this statement, when it is fully understood by couples, will cause them to take a long, hard look at how they treat each other. As nice as the compliments were from all of Jake's friends and family, he most wanted to hear praise from Tammy. Of all the people Jake wanted to impress, Tammy was on top of the list. When that did not happen, Jake was deeply hurt and felt insignificant. What he did didn't seem to matter to Tammy at all. The fact is that most men define who they are by what they do. It provides for them a sense of importance and validation.

A man's greatest need is to be important. He wants to feel that he makes a difference and that what he does matters. He wants to be appreciated and valued. Though many have a tough outward appearance, the

> **A man's greatest need is to be important.**

truth is, they still have a deep need to feel they have a purpose to accomplish in life. And when they accomplish it, they need to be recognized for it. Though the need to feel important and valued is primarily seen in men, many women share this need as well.

This is precisely what resulted for Adam. He had lost his position of importance as king of Eden and then had a deep longing to get it back. He wanted to feel that importance in position once again. If you have ever been frustrated at your attempts to succeed in something and failed then you can readily identify with the pain of feeling unimportant. In the arena of marriage, feelings of insignificance can lead to marital bust. A wife seeks to have her needs met by her husband. When this does not occur, she not only gets discouraged and demanding, but her husband feels defeated. Why? Because in his futile attempts to meet her needs and thus feel important, he fails.

Yet man was never created with the capacity to fully meet his wife's needs, and therefore, as he tries and fails, he becomes more defeated. Typically after a period of failures he will quit trying altogether and shut down emotionally in the relationship. No man with the innate need to feel valued and important will continually put himself in positions to fail. As with a woman's need for intimacy, no earthly relationship can fully meet a man's need for importance.

Men, God left the void in your life so that you would let Him fill that need with Himself. He can strengthen you in the deepest recesses of your heart. Unfortunately, you think you know of other things that will fill you so you stuff your hearts with all the wrong things. If you can accomplish enough in the work world, have enough money, live in bigger houses, drive nicer cars, own a boat, be the best on the golf course or at the hunting lodge, have the most trophies, or even get into another relationship, somehow, some way, these things will make you important. Jesus Christ is the only One who

> **God left the void in your life so that you would let Him fill that need with Himself.**

can satisfy the deep longing in your soul to find importance, value, and worth.

The summer before Jena's senior year in high school, she had a horrible automobile accident. Because of her injuries she was rushed straight to the emergency room for immediate attention. Her mother and father hurried to the hospital as soon as they heard the news. As her mother stood over Jena's bed, she made this simple but life-changing statement: "God left you on this earth for a purpose. You had best find out what it is and do it with all of your heart." God has a plan for *your* life. You are an important part of His plan. He has left you on this earth for a purpose. You had best find out what it is and do it with all of your heart.

Now women, don't think that this gets you off the hook either! With this curse on the men comes a calling for you as well. You have the wonderful privilege of pointing your husband to the One who made Him important in the first place. It is imperative that your husband know that you appreciate what he does for you and your family, but more importantly that God sees great value in him. Don't miss the opportunity to be grateful by verbally recognizing your husband's hard work and sacrifice for you. And point him to the very One who can give Him spiritual value and direction for your family now and in the future.

Luke 12:24 describes how important you are to Almighty God. You are more valuable than anything else God created! He has incredible plans for you (Jeremiah 29:11). And all the work you do that seems to be meaningless toil becomes full of meaning when we realize that all of it comes from the generous hand of God (Ecclesiastes 2:17-26).

When you finally realize that chasing after things does not fill your need for significance, you will run to the Need-Meeter, Jesus. From the very moment of your creation God has had plans for you, and His plans are for your good. There is not a single bird that falls to the ground that our Father does not know about. And how much more important are you to Him than a bird?

You were created with a purpose. Just think: God has wonderful plans for our lives that are one obedient, submissive step away yet many times we are too stubborn and self-reliant to follow Him. Will you commit yourself to seek God's intimate and important purpose for your life? Will you let Him fill that void? Make yourself available for His plans and you will begin an incredible journey with your Savior.

Vicious Cycle

So, we have come to recognize our need for intimacy and importance as individuals and have discovered how Christ is the only One who can meet those needs. Yet when we seek other ways to meet our needs, we get caught in a vicious cycle that too many times spins out of control.

> **When we seek other ways to meet our needs, we get caught in a vicious cycle that too many times spins out of control.**

In our marriage, this cycle was spinning faster than you can imagine. Jena had a tremendous need to be needed and loved. When I (Dale) did not fully meet that need, she went to church and taught a Bible study. After all, the women at church loved her and needed her to encourage and help them. Jena began to spend so much time with the women of her Bible study that I began to feel that I was moving down Jena's totem pole of priority and importance. So I headed to the golf course. There I could compete, accomplish something by attempting to win all the matches, and thus feel good about myself. Jena saw that I was spending more time at the golf course than with her so she began to feel that I didn't love her and was not committed to her. She began pouring her life into singing and writing musicals . . . busy, busy, busy. I assumed that I was not important to her anymore so I headed to the office to climb the corporate ladder. After all, the people there acknowledged my efforts and affirmed me for a job well done. And the cycle went on and on. Jena even recalls her thoughts at the birth of our first child, Cole: "Well, maybe when Dale sees the pain I go through to give him a son, he will love me more."

Do you see the neediness and the desperate measures we took to fulfill our needs? This vicious cycle of neediness is going on in households all over the world today, creating marital bust in dynamic proportions. With little concern for the other person's feelings, we continue in an effort to take care of ourselves and to meet our own needs which seem to drive us with a continual need for more. And without verbally saying it, our actions express that if somebody was hurt in the process, *Who cares? It's all about me.*

We learned through our divorce that all we had was Jesus and He was all we needed. His love, His goodness, His presence is the only thing that can fill the deep crevices of our lives and make us healthy and whole. When we learned that, we were able to minister to each other, pointing each other to the "Need Meet-er."

Freedom: Stopping the Cycle

When we were children, we definitely would have said that the icing is the best part of the cake. As adults, however, the best part has become the cake and not the icing. Icing just happens to be a little sweet extra that comes along with the cake.

As we allow Christ to fill the neediness in our lives, we no longer stretch out to our spouse, starving for love, affirmation, intimacy, and importance. When Christ fills those areas in our lives, He becomes the foundation, or the "cake", of our hearts. The encouragement, affirmation, love, and acceptance from our mate is wonderful and welcomed, but it is not what we stake our lives on. It becomes a nice addition to the fullness we already experience in and through Christ. Soon your favorite part becomes the cake, and the icing you receive from your mate is just the sweet, added extra.

You can be free from the demands of your mate's neediness because Christ is meeting his or her needs. You just offer extra encouragement. You can be free from disappointment when your mate is not meeting your needs because you no longer expect him or her to be the primary person who meets your needs. Your spouse is the "icing on the cake". And finally, you are free from feelings of defeat that come when your mate doesn't meet your expectations. When both you and your spouse are daily filling yourselves with Christ, you can each be free to love, encourage, and affirm each other out of devotion, not out of duty. Doesn't that sound like freedom to you?

Shame, blame, and pain took us down a road toward marital bust that we never dreamed we would travel. Friend, if you have found that your marriage is not what you bargained for, see if the characteristics of marital bust have found a place to lodge in your home. Ask your heavenly Father to tear down those areas that have crept into your life. Let God do His continuing work in your life and in the life of your spouse. Ground your marriage in the elements of marital bliss, founded on the perfect life of Christ. You can be confident in His working as you allow Him to refine you. Then your relationship can be above and beyond what you ever could have imagined. That is God's desire for our homes.

Jesus told us in Matthew 7:9-11 that God knows what we need and gives good gifts to us, His children. He gives us all that we need to do what He has called us to do (2 Corinthians 9:8). He supplies all our needs because He is rich (Philippians 4:19). And He offers us all the gracious blessings He has in our time of need (Hebrews 4:16).

Galatians 5:1 says, *"It is for freedom that Christ has set us free."* Christ came to set us free from sin and death, and so that we would not remain enslaved to the neediness of others. When we allow Christ to satisfy our deepest longings for intimacy and importance, we not only set our spouses free from the burden of meeting our needs but we also experience freedom from our own cravings of neediness and are empowered to minister His love, compassion, and kindness to others.

LET'S GET REAL

A Look at Our Legacy

"His divine power has given us everything we need for life and godliness through our knowledge of him who called us by his own glory and goodness. Through these he has given us his very great and precious promises, so that through them you may participate in the divine nature and escape the corruption in the world caused by evil desires" (2 Peter 1:3-4).

When we got married the first time, we honestly had no clue what we were getting into. At the tender ages of 21 and 22, we just knew we loved each other, that everybody else was getting married, and so were we. We certainly didn't know how our enemy Satan operated and how our family upbringing both developed and defined us. These two things had an incredible impact on our marriage. The enemy really used the formidable years of our lives—the homes we were raised in, the experiences we had, and the life we lived before getting married—to attack us in our way of relating.

The Enemy

Whether you believe it or not, you have an enemy who is against you and your marriage. His ONLY goal is utter ruin for you and your home, and he will stop at nothing until he reaches that goal.

> **You have an enemy who is against you and your marriage.**

But friend, don't lose heart. Remember, God's Word promises us that we are overcomers through Jesus Christ our Lord!

"The thief comes to kill, steal, and destroy, but I have come to give you life and to give it to you in its fullness" (John 10:10). In reading John 10:10, you understand that God's Word tells us that the thief, Satan, comes to steal, kill, and destroy. Have you ever thought about what exactly it is that Satan is trying to kill, steal, and destroy? The answer is found in the last part of the verse. Your enemy is trying to kill, steal, and destroy the abundant life Christ offers. Make no mistake about it. If you are a child of the King, you have an enemy who will do whatever he can to steal your joy, kill your passion, and destroy your marriage. Satan knows that a Christ-centered marriage is the world's picture of Christ's relationship as the Bridegroom to His Church, the Bride (Ephesians 5:31-32). He knows that if you get this marriage thing right, there is an entire generation to follow who will also get it right—a generation of godly Christian couples who will demonstrate what godly Christian, full-of-life marriages looks like.

The Enemy's Strategy

Once we learned about our root needs, intimacy and importance, we began to understand how Satan had attacked our minds. He had deceived us into thinking other things could meet those needs and fill the void in our lives, holes that only Christ could fill. Lies, facades of intimacy, and accusations are the ways of the enemy. He lies to us about who we are and who God is. He is a scheming snake, seeking ways to divide and destroy us. This is why we are told in Ephesians 6:11 to *"Put on the full armor of God so that you can take your stand against the devil's schemes."* So while Satan does not deserve our focus and attention, we shouldn't underestimate or ignore his plots against the children of God.

> **We shouldn't underestimate or ignore Satan's plots against the children of God.**

We believe that the enemy's strategy works something like this. We enter the world with needs. The enemy deceives us into thinking that other people or things will meet those needs. We exchange the truth of what will meet our needs (Christ) for the enemy's lies. Proverbs 23:7 says, *"As he thinks in his heart, so is he"* (NKJV). We begin to behave in ways that reflect our belief in the lie. Before we know it, Satan has a stronghold in our lives. We are slaves to the never-ending quest to fill our neediness, and are thus no longer free to enjoy the abundant life God has planned for us. The diagram below depicts the path the enemy uses.

Needs → Deception → Lie → Behavior → Stronghold

Maybe the lie you have accepted as truth is, *If I could just make a little more money, then I would feel important and valuable around here* or *If I could just look like that movie star or model, then I would be loved and accepted*. These are lies that can so consume you and your behavior that they become your focus, and you lose sight of God in the process. Remember, the enemy is after the abundant life offered by Christ. This is why he wants you to be so wrapped up in your stuff that you lose sight of your heavenly Father altogether.

Getting to the Root

As we share how we were reared, the influences in our lives before we got married, and the lies the enemy used in our lives to neutralize our marriage, we pray that the Spirit of God will reveal some lies that may have been passed down to you. Please note that this is not a parent-bashing chapter. It is not intended to degrade your family heritage in any way. God's Word plainly tells us to honor our parents that our days may be long (Exodus 20:12). You may have wonderful attributes in your family which are beautiful legacies to pass from generation to generation. There are also some characteristics that are not so admirable. Our goal for you is the same we have for ourselves—to see how the enemy has lied to us and to remove these lies from our lives and replace them with the truth of God's Word and the characteristics of Christ. Isn't it an incredible thought that God could use you to defeat some lies that have been passed from generation to generation, holding your family captive? This is why Christ came, that you might know Him and His truth so that you would be free (John 8:32; Luke 4:18-19). We have all been held captive by the lies of the enemy and felt downtrodden by his deceit, but your Father sent His Son to set you free. And he whom the Son sets free is free indeed (John 8:36)!

> **Isn't it an incredible thought that God could use you to defeat some lies that have been passed from generation to generation, holding your family captive?**

In our quest for freedom, the Lord began to show us, as a couple and as individuals, how He had been working and teaching us since we were children. He began bringing memories back from our pasts to give us a second chance at what Proverbs calls "wisdom and understanding". He reminded Jena of a time when she was growing up. Her grandparents, Nannie and James Mathis, lived on a farm in Pavo, Georgia. She loved to go to their house and see all of the fruits and vegetables that were reaped from the seeds sown months before.

One day, Grandpa James told Jena about apples on his apple tree. He said that when a flower buds forth on an apple tree, an apple would soon be formed. Many times, however, a worm attaches itself to the flower bud. Then the fruit of the apple grows around the bud or seedling, engulfing the worm with it. So when you see a hole in an apple, it is not that the worm has worked its way in, but it has worked its way out! This is what has happened to many of us. As children, the enemy, like a worm, has attached a lie to the seedling or bud of our hearts. The fruit, or behavior, of our lives has grown around that lie.

This is why a "tip and technique" approach to marriage never works for a sustainable period of time. Especially when there are deep-seated issues that must be rooted out first. We may try various methods to fix or clean up the fruit of our lives. We may even work on communication or our problems with anger, depression, eating disorders, performance, and perfectionism. The list could go on and on. While it's admirable to work on these things, life change will rarely occur until we deal with the root of our problems. Many of these behaviors are mere "fruit" that stem from a "worm" attached to the root in our lives. Romans 11:16 says that if our roots are holy, then the rest of us is holy. We must take the time to dig out the bad roots and replace them with the good.

> **Life change will rarely occur until we deal with the root of our problems.**

Jena's Lie—The 99 Syndrome

Right now, ask the Holy Spirit to reveal to you the lies that you have never been able to see. Again, if we can dig out the root lies and replace them with truth, then our lives—and thus our marriage—can bear good fruit that comes from good roots. For us, we had to have a deliberate and intentional partnership with the Holy Spirit because initially we couldn't see the lies. They had become such a regular pattern of our behavior. But the more intentional—even desperate—we became to get rid of the lies, the more revelation the Holy Spirit brought to us. We resolved that until we found the lies that were eating at the root of our hearts and replaced them with truth, we were never going to develop good, deep roots and live the abundant life offered by Christ. Perhaps you will identify with our discoveries.

I (Jena) grew up in a loving home with wonderful Christian parents who taught me the value of church, servanthood, and commitment. I was confident that God would provide because my father and mother worked very hard and sacrificed to provide for me. Though I had such a good upbringing, I had one "worm" attached to my heart: I was not very confident in myself. From an early age, I felt that I was not good enough. I can remember times in my life when I made a 99 on a math test and felt that I should have made 100. Feeling that my parents would be disappointed in my lack of perfection, I struggled to be the best but the feeling stayed the same. I was just a 99 . . . not quite good enough.

When I was a small child, the enemy began to fuel these thoughts. He fed my thought-life with continual belittling and condemnation about my less-than-acceptable and less-than-perfect life. These feelings eventually caused me to question God and His love for me. I bought into the lie that I wasn't good enough, and my behavior reflected it. I can remember playing on the playground with my best friend and watching another girl come along and take my friend away. The enemy taunted me in my thinking: "You're just not good enough. If you were, your friend would have stayed with you!" I remember the one beauty pageant I entered. I was awarded "Miss Congeniality". The attacks of the enemy ran through my mind as the deceptive voice of Satan cried out, "Jena, you're not quite good enough. If you were, you would have won this pageant." I remember striving so hard to graduate #1 in my class and being #9. Again I was not quite good enough. I not only believed the lie, but I began looking for affirmations of the lie in my life. Soon it became a stronghold for Satan—the stronghold of approval and performance. I so wanted the approval of others and of God that I did whatever anybody wanted me to do and tried desperately to be the best. If I was the best at everything I did, I felt I could somehow win their approval and love (my primary need). I thought that love from others and God was strictly conditional upon my actions. And though I worked hard and gained the approval of some, I was miserable on the inside, exhausted from the struggle and stronghold of people-pleasing performance. The enemy really used these lies in my life's journey prior to marriage and wrapped me in a stronghold I call the "99 Syndrome". It held me captive for 27 years of my life. And though I didn't realize it, it even impacted my marriage.

Dale's Lie—The Competitor's Syndrome

I (Dale) also grew up in a Christian home where I was taught the value of church, hard work, and fairness. The unique thing about my life is that I am an identical twin. As a twin, I was never my own person. I wasn't an individual; I was a "twin." In response to this, I learned quickly the importance of competing to be number one. I had to fight for my own identity. You see, if I was better at everything, then that would make me valuable, stand out, be noticed not for being a twin but for my successes and accomplishments. So I competed to be number one in baseball, basketball, golf, girls, grades, and popularity. As I continued my competition quest, the enemy took advantage of this opportunity to lie to me. After all, my number one need to feel important would only be validated when I competed and succeeded above everybody else. I bought into the lie that I had to be the best at everything, or at least be better than my twin brother, in order to be valuable and important. Everything I did either supported or confirmed the lie. This carried over into my view of God. I thought that I had to compete for God's love—to be perfect and successful in order to be loved and accepted by Him. The enemy really used these lies to deceive me. The result was a hard-charging husband with an unhealthy and deceptive need for approval. Jena found herself married to a man wrapped up in a stronghold of self-sufficiency that I call the "Competitor's Syndrome."

> I bought into the lie that I had to be the best at everything in order to be valuable and important.

Perhaps, you can identify with our journey. Or perhaps you have another lie that you have accepted as truth from the father of lies. Here is a list of potential lies and strongholds you might have accepted as truth:

"I must be perfect to be loved."
"I am unloved, unworthy, unacceptable."
"I am inadequate with nothing to offer."
"My past is too big to be free from."
"There's nothing special about me."
"I will always be this way."
"I don't need anyone. The only thing I need is me."
"God may work for you, but not for me."

Maybe you grew up believing that the only way to be accepted and loved was by looking pretty, and you have found yourself obsessed with your outer appearance or trapped by anorexia or bulimia. Maybe you are caught in an addiction to food, alcohol, or another substance. Or perhaps you learned at an early age that possessions bring happiness, and you are totally dependent on what you own to make you feel like you have worth. Even now, we pray for God to show you the lies so that you can uproot them and they can no longer hold you hostage. We pray that you will allow Jesus to re-plant His truth in your life.

Studying Your Family Tree

Not only do lies from the enemy cause us to have an unhealthy view of ourselves and of God, but also our family histories, both good and bad, have a profound effect on how we relate to others. Studying our families of origin allowed us to identify the struggles and stresses that occurred in our marriage because of family dynamics. It also helped us to see wonderful Christ-like character that was modeled before us that we would like to pass on to the generations coming after us. For much of what we saw, it wasn't that one family was right and the other wrong; they were many times simply different. And those differences caused some major issues for us. However, once we saw those differences, it helped us to understand each other much better and to learn how to adapt and work through them.

A LOOK AT OUR LEGACY

When we began this process of digging into our family history, we started by drawing our family trees, starting with our grandparents and moving down to ourselves (see below).

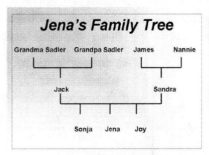
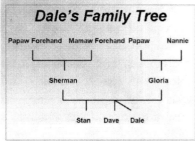

In the space provided below, draw your family tree. Your family tree may not look just like ours. Perhaps you were adopted, lived in foster care, raised by a single parent or grandparent. The point is for you to look for those people who most influenced your life and upbringing.

Once our tree was drawn, we began to write down the characteristics of each person on the tree. We described how they impacted us, their communication patterns, responses to conflict or stresses, repeated patterns of behavior. Suddenly we began to see how many of these habits, coping mechanisms, and attitudes had been passed down to us. Some of these qualities and characteristics were causing some differences and conflicts between us. Not that either person's upbringing was better, right, or wrong—they were just different. The enemy loves to enhance our differences and drive a wedge within our relationship.

> **The enemy loves to enhance our differences and drive a wedge within our relationship.**

We now want you to take some time, asking the Holy Spirit for revelation, to come up with descriptions of the influential people represented on your family tree. Here are some potential characteristics that have served as either negative or positive influences in your life:

Affectionate	Workaholic	Open Spiritually
Affirming	Private	Private Spiritually
Matter of Fact	Open	Church Attendee
Non-affectionate	Social	Anti-Church
Touchy-feely	Anti-social	Spender
Happy-go-lucky	Manipulative	Saver
Distant	Abusive	Impulsive
Engaging	Self-centered	Rigid
Non-engaging	Servant hearted	Flexible
Angry	Humble	Internal Processor
Peace-Maker	Teachable	External Processor
Quiet and Reserved	Rebellious	Caretaker
Loud and Outgoing	Dictatorship	Clown
Avoided Conflict	Agreeable	Giver
Open Conflict		
Non-affectionate		

Think about questions like these: Who influenced you the most as a child? How are you like that person? How are you different? How did you see conflict handled? What was the solution, if any? How did you react to it? How did you see your parents or guardians interact with each other? Did they spend frequent time together or very little time together?

Our Family Trees: Jena's Tree

My paternal grandparents were very work-oriented and maintained high levels of commitment to both church and family. They taught my father the value of knowing and loving God's Word and being very active and committed to the church. My grandfather loved Coke and peanuts and always had some available for our family when we came to visit. He loved a good laugh. Because of their influence, my father grew into a hard worker with strong commitments, who was funny, and who was a wonderful provider.

My maternal grandparents were also very hard workers and were very service-oriented. They were friendly and liked to be around people. They lived on a farm and helped many people in their community who were in need. Both of my maternal grandparents died during our divorce, which brought me face to face with the certainty of death and the brevity of life. At their funerals, people I did not know came to me sharing what my grandparents had done for them. My grandparents had received no accolades, no applause; they just did good things for those around them because they loved as Christ loves. Because of their example, my mother is a very loving, fun, affectionate, giving person. What a sobering thought to think that children become what they see day in and day out.

> **What a sobering thought to think that children become what they see day in and day out.**

When my parents had conflict, they talked it out until it was resolved. Their motto was don't let the sun go down on your wrath. So they worked hard at a resolution even if it took all night. They also spent the majority of their time together.

So I came into our marriage believing that I was a 99 (not quite good enough), confident that I would always be provided for and willing to give and serve when I saw a need. I also shared my parents' value of laughter and loving God's Word. Finally, I thought that during times of conflict everything should be talked out and that Dale and I should spend all of our time together. After all, that is what happened in my home—and everybody's home looked the same, right?

Our Family Trees: Dale's Tree

My paternal grandparents were all about ministry. My grandfather was a Baptist preacher committed to ministering to others. Many people have told me how he spoke the Word of God boldly and unashamedly. Today I share his passion for preaching and teaching the Word in ministry to others.

My father was the oldest of five children so he felt responsible for leadership and keeping peace in the home in his father's absence. My father was the ultimate peacemaker, a trait he learned from his family environment.

My maternal grandparents were some of the hardest-working people in America. They married during the height of the Depression and learned the value of hard work and partnership. They were very service-oriented and giving. I can tell many stories about the joys of playing in my grandmother's backyard and of her having candy waiting for me when I got off the school bus. The attention she gave me made me feel like I was the most important person in the world. My mother thus became a hard-working and giving person just like her parents. She showed her love through service to her children just as she had seen her mother do.

My parents brought their histories with them into their marriage. I never saw conflict in my home because my father was the peacemaker. My parents worked incredibly hard during the week so they spent the weekends doing things they enjoyed, like playing golf and serving the family. Many times they simply did their own thing, very rarely together.

Can you see the similarities of faith and family priority in the way we were raised? Can you also see how differently we were raised? When we realized these differences, we gained a completely different perspective of our marriage. Jena came in with a need for affirming words that told her *You are a 100, You are beautiful, I love you.* She expected to talk through our conflicts and spend most of our time together. I came into the marriage with a need to feel valued and important. I also desired physical affection from Jena. I did whatever it took to keep the peace and wanted time away to do my own thing. Are you beginning to see why we had struggles in our marriage?

Joined Together

Our first year of marriage was difficult as we tried desperately to get the other to meet our needs. When conflict arose, Jena wanted to talk it out and I (Dale) wanted to go to bed in hopes that tomorrow would be a better day. When I went to bed, it confirmed to Jena that she must be a 99 because if I really loved her, I would stay up and talk it out. The sad thing is that I had no idea what I was communicating through my actions—that I was damaging the relationship. I just thought I had to work hard, provide for my family, and keep the peace.

At one point that first year, we had a major disagreement. As the fight escalated, I (Dale) chose to go to bed. This was one of the ways I sought to keep peace (at least then we weren't fighting). Jena got frustrated and left the house. She drove all over town until 2 a.m. When she finally returned home, I was fast asleep. For the little girl who thought she was a 99, I just affirmed the lie as truth. What does someone struggling with the "99 Syndrome" want a spouse to do? Jena wanted me to summon the police, call her mother and father, wake up the pastor, send out the bloodhounds, and do whatever it took to find her. Why? Because she was worth it! Jena desired, even longed for confirmation that she was a 100-plus in my life. She, like so many wives, wanted me to demonstrate that I valued her as my bride and gift from God. When that did not occur, the pain was intense, the lie confirmed, and the stronghold continued.

Do you see what happened? It was not that Jena's ways were right and mine wrong or that Jena's ways were wrong and mine right. They were simply different. Our neediness and ignorance of our family dynamics caused deeply injured feelings, captivity to the lies of the enemy, and strongholds of behavior. Our marriage was not free; it was in bondage! From these discoveries came the opportunity to make some changes based on our new understanding of each other. Now whenever conflict arises in our home, I (Jena) know that although I want to talk it out, Dale will need time to think about it and to possibly cool off. So to minister to each other, I now offer Dale the time he needs, and he will tell me the time that we can get back together to talk it out. You see, we are considering our differences in upbringing and ministering to each other rather than demanding our own way.

> **From these discoveries came the opportunity to make some changes based on our new understanding of each other.**

Our backdrop of experiences, our family dynamics, the good and the not-so-good things we have witnessed have a huge impact on our relationships. We pray that the Holy Spirit is turning on some lights for you to see some truths that have been hidden from view in your life and marriage.

In Your Marriage

How has the enemy been holding your marriage captive to the lies he has fed you? How has your family of origin affected your marriage? When the Holy Spirit begins to shine His Light into our lives, we are set free from the dark, hidden areas and the deceptive lies of the enemy. John 1:4–5 says, *"In Him was life, and that life was the light of men. The light shines in the darkness, but the darkness has not understood it."* The darkness cannot overcome the light. Through Christ, we see a life that was a light for us to live by. Do you know where freedom from the enemy comes from? It comes from walking in the light of Christ.

For some, digging deep into the recesses of your hearts and homes may be easy. For others, it may be the toughest and most painful experience you've ever had. Facing a difficult and painful past is never easy. Our fleshly nature desires to leave it there, push it back down when it attempts to resurface, or pretend it never happened. Yet to truly be set free, we must remove the bad roots that are bearing bad fruit in our marriage. Can this happen? Is it even possible? We want to encourage you by sharing what God did to release us from the enemy's snare. First, there was one requirement, and that was to cooperate with Him through obedience. Second Peter 1:3-10 says God has given us all we need for true life and godliness but we also must do our part to make every effort to live out His character, His truth.

Tearing Down the Strongholds

As we discovered the lies and sought to destroy them, God took us on a path toward healing and wholeness in close communion with the Holy Spirit. He showed us three things we had to do in order to tear down the strongholds in our lives. We quickly learned that this was not something we were to do only one time but is a daily choice as we embrace freedom.

The Bible urges us to put on the whole armor of God (Ephesians 6:11), and the first piece of armor is the belt of truth. The first thing we had to do was to **ACKNOWLEDGE** the lies that have held us captive. Just as an alcoholic must admit that there is a problem, we had to acknowledge the lies that we have accepted as truth.

We knew we couldn't do this alone. In fact, we were never designed to do so. Jesus says that apart from Him we can do nothing (John 15:5). That's why the second step in your journey to freedom has to be an **APPEAL** to God through prayer (Philippians 4:6–7). So many of us take for granted the privilege and the power of prayer. God longs for us to call out to Him. He doesn't need some boastful, embellished prayer. He just wants your heart in desperate need of His saving grace and truth. When we were going through our divorce, I (Jena) can remember climbing into the red bunk bed night after night with our son Cole and crying myself to sleep. Many nights, prayers went before the Lord from a wounded heart, and they were as simple as *Help me*. No doubt these simple, short prayers were the most precious prayers ever prayed for they were prayed from a heart that had come to the end of itself and had come begging the Father to help. I (Dale) remember night after night as I approached our house that once was a home, praying, "God, go before me; I don't think I can do this anymore." In the helpless, hopeless moments, we must appeal to our Heavenly Father. He longs to hear from us and He longs to help us.

After we acknowledged our strongholds and appealed to God in prayer, it was time for us to **ADOPT** a new way of thinking—to obey His Word. Picture a tape recorder in your brain playing lies over and over again until you've accepted them as truth. This is exactly what happened to us. Jena continually heard, "You're a 99 and will always be a 99." Jena expected things to turn out a certain way because of her false belief system. And the tape continued to play. My (Dale's) lie played continuously in my mind as well, saying, "I will win at whatever cost." We had to stop the tape, take it out, and replace it with the truth. This was a process. We had lived these lies for many years, and we had to intentionally strive to practice believing and walking in our newfound truth—the truth God had for us.

We had to remember: "Jena, you're not a 99; you are a 100-plus—not because of anything good in you, but because My Son lives in you." "Dale, you don't have to be perfect. You don't have to win to be important. You are important because I sent My Son to die for you. You are important to Me and My Kingdom."

It was time for God's truth to become our new way of thinking and living. We had no idea how to begin this quest for truth so we decided to get up every morning and simply ask God this question: "What do You think of me? Would You guide me into all truth?" God walked us through the pages of His Word and daily showed us just what He thought of us. Here are just a few of the Scriptures God brought before us: Genesis 1:26; Psalm 56:8; Jeremiah 29:11; Philippians 4:13; Matthew 19:26; Isaiah 43:1–5. Take some time to look up these Scriptures in your Bible. Let them sink down deep in your soul and take root in the soil of your heart.

> **It's time for God's truth to become your new way of thinking and living.**

The words of our Father, Savior, and Friend continued to pour over us like fresh water to quench our sick and thirsty souls. His Word began to sweep over us and change our outlook and behavior, freeing us from the lies that held us. We found the truth, and that Truth set us free (John 8:32). The truth of Christ destroyed the enemy's hold over us. We were no longer in bondage to the lies that affected our marriage, preventing us from ministering to a lost and dying world. Our adversary was defeated! The blood of Jesus Christ and the word of our testimony defeated him! (Revelation 12:11).

As we began to believe and live in the truth about ourselves, God began to turn our hearts towards each other with greater compassion and understanding. We realized that our behavior toward each other was a response budding forth from either a lie we'd lived in, or by the way we were raised. We stopped blaming each other and stopped wondering what was wrong with us because we were so different from each other. We actually started understanding the whys behind our behavior and began to help each other and to work through our differences with compromises and unity. God can do this for your marriage too if you will stop making excuses for yourselves and allow Him to change you from the inside out.

For each of us there comes a day of reckoning—a day when we can no longer blame our past on the failures of others. There comes a day when we must take a step toward freedom's path, acknowledging our strongholds, appealing to God in prayer, adopting a new way of thinking, and living in the freedom Christ offers. Friend, there is victory in Jesus! Don't let the enemy have a hold over you any longer. You can be free in Jesus Christ—free from the lies, free from the pain of past sin, free from your past struggles, free from your differences, and free to glorify Him through your life and marriage. Hallelujah, what a Savior!

THE SHAME TRAIN

> *"Praise be to the God and Father of our Lord Jesus Christ, the Father of compassion and the God of all comfort, who comforts us in all our troubles, so that we can comfort those in any trouble with the comfort we ourselves have received from God" (2 Corinthians 1:3-5).*

During our journey toward reconciliation, God opened our eyes to see many things we had not seen before. We were amazed at what the Holy Spirit was revealing to us about ourselves, our upbringing, our needs, our motives, and our hearts. Some of it was good but some of it was despicable. As we began to see the sin that was penetrating our hearts and lives, God gave us a new perspective of ourselves.

Like uneaten leftovers in our refrigerator, we often allow sin to take up residence in our hearts until it rots. When we allow the enemy to deceive us with his slant on the sin in our lives, he distorts our way of thinking by flooding our minds with shame.

Shame is a real emotion. It is a feeling that everybody else is normal and okay, but you are not. It's not just that you make a mistake or do something wrong; shame says there is something wrong with you—with who you are—that you are defective

> **Shame makes you feel that damage has been done to the deepest part of who you are and cannot be repaired.**

physically, mentally, or emotionally while everybody else has it all together. Shame makes you feel that damage has been done to the deepest part of who you are and cannot be repaired.

There is a huge difference between conviction over sin and shame from our sin. Conviction says, "My behavior was wrong, but I am still a normal person. I made a mistake and need to confess, repent, and move forward with God." Shame says, "I am a mistake. I am abnormal. I mess up all the time, and I just can't get it together. Everybody else can get it right, but not I. There is something wrong with me. God must be disgusted with me." Shame leaves people very defeated with no hope, but conviction can draw you to your Savior and take you even deeper in relationship with Him. Conviction leads to growth and newfound freedom. Yet many of us are still rotting in the devil's snare of shame.

Have you ever thought *if others really knew me they would not like me. If they really knew the sin that has been or is currently in my life, they would reject me?* If you have ever thought this then you are carrying shame in your life. The enemy is using it as a means to keep you captive.

Many may carry shame from sin that was self-inflicted. You sinned on your own accord, out of your own choosing. Still others may be carrying around shame from a sin that someone else inflicted upon them. They were sinned against. Regardless, shame can take root in your heart leaving you stagnant in your relationships.

As a child, I (Jena) had extremely yellow teeth because of a medicine I had to take. Many people began to call me Greena, a nickname that embarrassed me. For them it was all in jest but for a child who was just beginning to find her place as a young lady, it was a shaming experience. It was so shaming that I was extremely self-conscious about my teeth. I didn't show my teeth much even when I spoke or smiled.

> **Shame can take root in your heart leaving you stagnant in your relationships.**

Along with the shame I already felt came my own willful disobedience to God which carried consequences into adulthood. During our divorce trial, Dale and I accused, questioned, and blamed each other in an effort to obtain custody of our children.

There were accusations of affairs, child neglect, child abuse, and mental instability. Wounding words were hurled that cut to the core. The devastation and pain were indescribable. It was as if we were dreaming, hoping we hadn't really experienced these things. But it was no dream, and the wounds inflicted were deep.

The enemy added both my willful choices to sin, as well as the wounds from those who inflicted them, to bind me in the captivity of shame. He planted a seed of shame deep in my heart which took root and left me too wounded to love, give, or minister to others.

According to Acts 3:19, when we allow our sin to transform us instead of shaming us, God brings us times of refreshing. May God help us to not be taken by Satan's snare of shame over our sin or over the sin of others, but may we take these to the Lord who can wash over us and refresh us.

Instead of taking my shame to God, I felt that I was no good, worthless, and ruined for life. Many times feelings like these lead us down a road that God never intended for us to travel. Dale and I call it the "Shame Train."

The Elements of Shame

The "Shame Train" looks something like this:

Hurt *leads to*
    Anger *leads to*
        Bitterness *leads to*
            Shame *leads to* either
                Performance or Destruction

When we disobey God or when someone sins against us, our hearts are hurt. If we do not deal with that hurt but suppress it or ignore it in the hope that it will go away, we soon become angry. Sometimes we don't even recognize the source of our anger. We find ourselves angry for allowing sin into our lives. We find ourselves angry with others who might have prevented shameful experiences. Sometimes we are angry with God for allowing our sinfulness or the sinfulness of others. This soon leads us to bitterness—a ceaseless, continual focus on the hurt that leaves a constant bad taste in our mouths. Before we are even aware of it, we have become immensely depressed. We are staying in bed longer, dwelling on the hurt. We begin having warped thoughts as the enemy continues his deception and lies. Suddenly our behavior begins to reflect one of two extremes. We either begin to perform our way into feeling good about ourselves again or we begin to self-destruct through anger, control, and manipulation because we feel that there is no hope for restoration.

I (Jena) chose the road of performance. After all, I had already bought into the enemy's original lie that I was just a 99 and never measured up. Moving from shame to performance as an escape wasn't a big leap. I hoped to perform my way into the hearts of others and God through my new personality, intelligence, and appearance. But my hopes for happiness soon deteriorated as the condemning feelings still consumed my thinking. I wasn't sure who I was anymore because the old Jena had become lost in the newfound Jena that I had created. The voice inside me kept saying, "Because of all the woundedness and sin in my life, I have no value whatsoever." Soon I was convinced that God would always be disappointed in me. Therefore, I created a false self that would cover up who I once was since that person obviously did not measure up. Just like Adam and Eve, I created my own elaborate fig leaves. The enemy thought he had won.

Dale moved toward destruction. When feelings of shame and hurt cut him to the core, he came out fighting. His battle method was, "I will destroy whoever or whatever is not on my side." His mentality: "If I can somehow win and come out on top at the end of the day—be the one still standing—then I will be important and a success." Dale marched to the drumbeat of *If you're not for me then you're against me.* And this response was not a far leap since his upbringing and Satan's lies had already trapped him into becoming a competitive, highly charged personality.

The destruction in Dale's life showed up as a driving need to be in control, to have all the answers, and to be in charge. Because of hurt and anger which led to bitterness, Dale allowed the enemy to fuel the destruction with lies and deceit. And the more he pushed people, the more they walked away and left him alone. Depression set in as he realized he was not in control after all and didn't have all the answers. Believing that his importance came from this, Dale became void of emotion. He just emotionally shut down since his attempts to be in control were not working. Consequently, he continued on a pendulum path, swinging from forceful control to emotional numbness. His plan to destroy whoever or whatever got in his way ended up destroying him in the process. There was no victory in that at all.

For those who are having a difficulty with this chapter, God promises restoration and strength in 1 Peter 5:10–11. Though you may be suffering through this section, as painful as it may be, know that God will strengthen you through this, you will become steadfast in who you are, and no one will be able to shake you.

May God bring you much comfort in knowing that He is personally committed to your healing and restoration. His all-surpassing power and grace will grant you healing and strength as you journey through this difficult process with Him.

Understanding Our Shame

The word shame appears in various forms throughout Scripture, the Greek and Hebrew carrying similar definitions. However, one defining word that continually appears within the definitions is confusion. As we began to study and ask for the Holy Spirit's guidance towards truth and understanding, God allowed us to understand this reality: as we travel farther on the shame train, we forget who God created us to be. We become confused about who we really are because we're so consumed by the shame we feel before God and others.

Yet who do we know is the author of confusion? The enemy himself. Satan holds us captive in our shame by confusing us about who we are. He causes us to question ourselves and God. And what did the enemy use to cause Adam and Eve to stumble into their sin? He caused them to question God's command. He began to enslave them through doubt and confusion. And in the end they were ashamed. The enemy still uses the same old strategy today, shaming believers into captivity.

> **We become confused about who we really are because we're so consumed by the shame we feel before God and others.**

Consider a woman who grew up in a home with sexual abuse or was raped earlier in her life. Sometimes the intense hurt that mars her heart puts her on the shame train, and she doesn't even know it. She continually struggles with her weight and cannot understand why then she realizes that her addiction to food is a response to her immense shame. In order to protect herself from further physical abuse, she becomes overweight. She makes this agreement with the enemy: "If I am unattractive to men, they won't hurt me." The shame train brings her to self-destruction and confusion.

Or think about a wife who finds that her husband is addicted to pornography and has had multiple affairs. She begins to travel on the shame train. She questions why she is not good enough or pretty enough. She moves from immense hurt to anger, then bitterness and depression, and then finds herself on the fast track down the performance street. She begins to be obsessed with her weight, her body, her clothes, her make-up, her hairstyle, and her sensuality. The confusion over who she really is begins a cycle of depression and performance that is never-ending.

These are some of the paths where shame can take us. It is an intense stronghold, and it leads to other strongholds that keep us imprisoned personally and relationally.

Consider how men are conditioned by this world: *Big boys don't cry. I must control my own destiny. If we have good sex, we must have a good marriage. If I am a good provider for my family, that makes me a good husband.* These lies only lead to emptiness in a relationship. A husband who is dangerously driven toward climbing the corporate ladder to be a great provider—the captain of his own ship—may be harsh at home. He attempts to connect only physically with his wife. The wife who is now feeling emotionally empty doesn't respond the way he wants. He feels hurt which eventually leads to anger, bitterness, and possibly depression. The husband selfishly responds by either performing his way to reconnecting or stonewalling, manipulating his wife through the cold shoulder tactic, lashing out in anger, or causing destruction. If none of these tactics work, he will just quit all together or find himself in an affair that gives him a temporary good feeling about himself.

> Shame is an intense stronghold, and it leads to other strongholds that keep us imprisoned personally and relationally.

The confusion over who he is results in his making agreements with the enemy: *because of my unmet need, I want others to hurt as badly as I do.* Destruction begins to occur in his relationships. As a result, his marriage deteriorates as the couple is separated emotionally. The shame in the relationship rises to new heights. It's amazing how self-centered we can become as we start operating with an *if you don't meet my needs, I'll punish you* mentality.

John 8:32 says that we will know the truth and the truth will make us free. We must know the truth about what Satan has done to deceive us through shame and the truth about what God says about us that counters his shaming tactics.

Consider Satan's deception and shame in Genesis 3. In verse 1 we find that Satan was more crafty than any other creature the Lord had made and he sought to cause Eve to doubt

God's heart toward her. With his comment he caused Eve to question whether God really cared about her or if He was holding something good from her. Satan then caused her to further doubt God when he contradicted God and told her that she would not die for eating the fruit.

Then verse 6 says, *"When the woman saw that the fruit of the tree was good for food and pleasing to the eye, and also desirable for gaining wisdom, she took some and ate it. She also gave some to her husband who was with her, and he ate it."* That word saw means convinced. Satan convinced Eve that he was right and God was wrong by appealing to Eve's flesh. He is still deceiving us the same way. And as soon as their eyes were opened, they sewed fig leaves around them to hide their nakedness (their being found out). What fig leaves have you placed on yourself?

May God help us to see the way that the enemy has confused us about who we are and what God thinks of us due to sin and wounds in our lives. May His constant, unconditional love allow us to remove the fig leaves that we have hidden behind so He can forgive and heal us.

Are You on the Shame Train?

The summer before my senior year in high school, I (Jena) had a major car wreck. I suffered multiple internal and external wounds that took quite some time to heal. When the accident first occurred, I had no idea of the extent of my wounds. I was in shock. I really had no idea that I was hurt as badly as I was. But after reality set in and the doctors began to minister to my wounds, I recognized the severity of my injuries and my need for healing and rehabilitation. I had to learn to walk all over again. I went through a long and thorough process of training and therapy. Today all I am left with is a bunch of scars that tell me where I've been and where I never want to return.

If you have experienced shame, you may be in one of these three places:

- Maybe you are in shock. You would consider the possibilities of having shame in your life but you are unaware of the extent of your wounds. You have no idea how badly you have been wounded and how severely your wounds are affecting your life and relationships.
- You may recognize the origin of your shame and be on the road toward healing. You may have begun the process of re-training yourself in truth and re-embracing God's healing power over your life.
- Or you may be walking in complete victory over your shame, carrying nothing but scars from the pain that you endured in your past, reminding you of where you've been and where you never intend to go again.

Wherever you are, you can be assured that God does not want you to live your life in confusion about yourself due to sin or your being sinned against. Paul tells us in 1 Corinthians 14:33 that God is not a God of confusion, but of peace. He desires peace for you, not confusion.

When we first began to share our testimony at various churches, we would get extremely emotional as we proclaimed the gut-wrenching truths of what our lives had become. We were humbled, sometimes embarrassed, and even scared of how people would receive our painful story. However, the more we shared and saw God using our pain to help others, the easier it became to visit the hurt. Now we can share our scars openly. They aren't nearly as painful as the initial wounds, and God continues to use them to minister to hurting couples. That is the God we serve. He loves to take broken and marred vessels and use them to bring honor and glory

> **You can be assured that God does not want you to live your life in confusion about yourself due to sin or you being sinned against.**

to Himself. If we were perfect, unscarred vessels, we could do life apart from Him. Being marred and scarred, there is no doubt that God's hand is at work in and through us to bring Him glory.

When we look at the perfect example of our Savior, we see that it is because of His stripes and scars that we are healed. His scars are for our healing. Isaiah 53:3–5 tells us His scars saved us from our sin. Many who share their scars hope to save others from making the same mistakes that they have made. But we also have to look at John 20:24–29. There we see that Jesus shared His scars with others so that they would believe. He offered comfort, courage, and hope to those who were walking in the shame of their sin. His scars set us free from our sin. The price was paid. Today His scars are still being shared with all who will listen.

You see, friend, what the enemy intends for evil, God turns to good (Genesis 50:20). The scars in your life, whether self-inflicted or not, are not purposed to condemn you. They are not present for you to feel like you have no value or are unacceptable, unapproved of, and unloved. God's Word says that there is no condemnation for those who are in Christ Jesus (Romans 8:1). Instead, our scars' purpose is two-fold: (1) to grow us and strengthen us to be like Christ and (2) to comfort others. God wants to heal us in such a miraculous way in order to grow us and then to give us a powerful story to share of His incredible love. Following His example, we are to give others comfort, courage, and hope. In 2 Corinthians 1:3–5 we read, *"Praise be to the God and Father of our Lord Jesus Christ, the Father of compassion and the God of all comfort, who comforts us in all our troubles, so that we can comfort those in any trouble with the comfort we ourselves have received from God."*

Through our ministry, we have the privilege of meeting many of God's precious children. About two years ago we had the opportunity to begin encouraging a couple whose marriage was being torn apart due to an extramarital affair. We watched the woman go through pain, anger, frustration, hatred, revenge, depression, and more. She was deteriorating physically, emotionally, and spiritually right before our eyes. But God pulled this precious lady back up and set her feet firmly on the solid rock of her Savior. She and her marriage were healed by the pure grace of God. With new understanding, she experienced the reality of Psalm 40:1–3: *"I waited patiently for the Lord; He turned to me and heard my cry. He lifted me out of the slimy pit, out of the mud and mire; He set my feet on a rock and gave me a firm place to stand. He put a new song in my mouth, a hymn of praise to our God. Many will see and fear and put their trust in the Lord."*

Two years later this woman called us. The change in her voice was evidence enough that the Spirit had healed her and was controlling her life. In our conversation she began to share the road of shame that the enemy took her down and how quickly she had spiraled downward to her defeat and to his victory. Then she shared how Jesus had allowed her to understand the enemy's tactics. Miraculously God had set her free from the bondage of shame. When asked what had prompted her release from shame, she said that she had heard from an old friend who was going through a similar situation. She said that she had been able to encourage and help her friend to walk through the hardest time in her life. She then told us that she would never have known how to help that woman had she not gone through it herself two years earlier. At that moment God changed her heart and brought her to this conclusion: *My suffering can be used for somebody else's sake.*

Oh friend, do you see? Sovereign God wants us to share our scars in order to proclaim His mercy, His grace, His goodness, and His unfailing, never-ending, unconditional love. He wants your greatest misery to become your greatest ministry. When we allow the Holy Spirit to change our perspective about our sin from shame to scars, He allows our scars to comfort another.

May we follow Jesus' example and allow His power to heal us so that we can share our scars with others and they too can believe and be healed.

Getting Off the Train

While sharing our pain certainly provides a healing balm to our shame, there is another integral step in the healing process. We need to cleanse ourselves from the sin that caused the shame. If it was your sin that caused your shame, you must forgive yourself and allow Christ to forgive you.

> **If it was your sin that caused your shame, you must forgive yourself and allow Christ to forgive you.**

Have you repented and accepted the forgiveness of God provided through the shed blood of His only Son Jesus Christ? It is available to you, a free gift of grace, if you will ask. As a believer, it is as simple as saying, "Father God, I know that I have sinned against You and You only. I know that my sin separates me from fellowship with You. I recognize my need for forgiveness and humbly accept it as a sheer gift of grace—as nothing that I have done. I change my thinking about this area of sin in my life and I ask You, by the power of Your Spirit within me, to help me overcome this sin and to live a life that brings You pleasure and honor. In the name of the One who makes this possible, Jesus Christ. Amen." From here, you enter a partnership with God to work through, transform, and heal you from the inside out. It involves removing the lies and replacing them with truth, setting some good boundaries in your life to protect you from falling prey to the same sin, and walking so closely with God that you hear His voice telling you when to walk away from areas of temptation.

We found incredible freedom and peace with God as we took these steps towards forgiveness, repentance, and reconciliation. However, we also found that some people, even Christian people, did not believe us genuine. They continued to judge us and reject us. While we realized that it might take time for our behavior to offer proof of a real and lasting change, there were some who still would not offer us grace, love, or forgiveness, and it was very hurtful.

Are there people trying to keep your past sins alive—trying to hold you captive to sins that God has already forgiven? Are there people who you know will consider themselves judge and jury over you for the rest of your life?

Should anyone ever choose to judge you because of your past, understand this: they are really not questioning you; they're questioning the power of the blood of Jesus Christ to cleanse, heal, and cover sin. And if we as a people choose to cast stones at others' sin and shame then we are blinded by self-righteousness, not recognizing that we too sin. We also are making a mockery of the blood of Jesus. If we continue to hold people hostage to their sin, we are saying that the shed blood of Jesus was not enough to cover it. You go to God with your shame and confess your sin. Against Him and Him only have you sinned, and it is only from Him that you need forgiveness (Psalms 51:4). Accept His cleansing, covering blood, and walk away in freedom. Now certainly if your sin wounded someone else then it is imperative that you go to him or her and ask for forgiveness, and how you do that will be covered in a chapter to follow. But for now, we want to deal with our shameful, willful, disobedient sin against our heavenly Father and make that right. For without His forgiveness and help, we are bound to make the same sinful mistakes over and over again.

If the shame is from someone else's sin, give it back. If someone sinned against you and hurt you, don't take that sin on as yours! So many times we take other people's sin and shame upon ourselves and accept it

> **If the shame is from someone else's sin, give it back.**

as our own when it was never ours to begin with. Release the shame to its rightful owner. This does not in any way negate the wound or pain that was inflicted upon you because of their sinful actions. You were deeply wounded but your healing must be your focus, and that will take time and concentrated effort. Put others' sin back on them. They made their choices. You did not make them do anything; they chose. If you did have a part to play then make it right with them. If not then let it go. And do not let them convince you any longer that you made them do it. Nobody can make anybody do anything. We all get to choose.

As you journey toward healing and freedom, you will walk into a new dimension of which you never dreamed—the freedom of forgiveness. For some, forgiveness is not a word they can say, much less put into practice. The truth is, though, that a time will come when you are so healed and freed from your past that you learn not only to forgive yourself but to forgive your perpetrator even if you never hear the words *I'm sorry* from them. Sound foreign to you?

We can tell you that we have seen many people locked in someone else's shame. Many have been physically assaulted by another. They feel so guilty and ashamed of the incident that it begins to eat them up like a cancer. The perpetrator may feel no remorse at all while the victim is withering on the vine.

We witnessed this firsthand when we saw a lady sitting alone in the corner of a conference center where we had spoken. She was frail, weak, and looked near death. We spoke with her and found that she had had many years of marriage struggles. But the root of the problem was an event that struck their home years before. A man forced his way inside their house and raped this woman. This precious lady had held onto this shameful experience for many, many years until it had debilitated her beyond comprehension.

Her husband was dealing with his own shame. He had been a strong leader in our military and was called to duty, which left him absent when the rape occurred. The enemy had bound him in intense guilt over the fact that he was not there to protect his wife. If he had been present, she would not be suffering.

As we continued to speak with them, we shared how grateful we were that they felt safe enough with us to share their pain. We also encouraged them to go with their Abba Daddy on a journey of letting Him heal them, confident that one day God would use their story to help others. We then began to discuss the fact that the sin was not theirs to bear but was to be released to the one who had caused them these wounds and shame. From there we talked about the forgiveness of God and how we must accept His forgiveness and then bestow it on others. With a startled expression, the woman asked us, "Are you telling me that I have to forgive that man for what he did to me?"

We so did not want to inflict more pain, but after a long pause, our answer rang loudly, "Yes, ma'am, you do." Fear, anger, frustration, and pain oozed from the heart of this dear, sweet woman of God. Holding her as she wept before the Lord, we prayed for God to heal her heart and to take her on a journey to wholeness, then we headed for home.

When we reached Birmingham, we began to pray for this woman and her husband. We prayed that God would give her husband the ability to forgive himself for not being there for his wife. We prayed for him to have wisdom to come alongside and love his wife through this time. We prayed that he would be tender toward her. And we prayed that she would be released from her shame, that she would not hold it against her husband for his not being there for her, and that the two of them could lock arms and journey this road to healing together. Within a few weeks, we received a phone call at our home. We did not recognize the voice, but it was this dear, sweet lady. She sounded so different, so free. She told us that she had forgiven herself, had accepted the forgiveness of God, and had forgiven the man who hurt her. She shared that she did forgave the person not because he deserved it nor to exonerate him from his sin; rather she chose to forgive him for herself so that she could be released from the shame she had carried around for so long—shame that wasn't hers to bear. She was obeying God because He told her to forgive. Her husband had done the same. God restored their joy, their life, and their marriage.

> **Is shame keeping you from the abundant life God planned for you?**

In Galatians 6:4–5, Paul instructs us to test our actions and to only own the sin that is ours to own. Are you traveling on the shame train? Are you in bondage to your sin or to another's sin? Is shame keeping you from the abundant life God planned for you? There is freedom waiting for you at the foot of the cross. Lay down your shame today. Determine that sin and shame no longer have a place in your life. The blood of Jesus has covered you, and Satan has no place to accuse you anymore. Declare out loud that Satan has no place in this area of your life, that you have been forgiven, have forgiven, and are daily choosing to walk in freedom. Revelation 12:11 says, *"They overcame him [Satan] by the blood of the Lamb and by the word of their testimony."*

1 John 1:7 says, *"If we walk in the light, as He is in the light, we have fellowship with one another, and the blood of Jesus, His Son, purifies us from all sin."* Verse 9 goes on to say that *"If we confess our sin, God is faithful and just and will forgive our sins and cleanse us from all our unrighteousness."*

Finally, we are described in 2 Corinthians 4:7 as vessels who hold the incredible power of forgiveness through Christ, the gospel. May we be vessels of clay that though once marred are now healed to show the all-surpassing power of our great God.

In light of all that God has revealed to us, let's take some time with Him to look inwardly. Where are you in this area of shame? Would you be willing to go through the process of forgiveness for your own sin as well as the sin of another? If yes, we would love to hear about your journey to freedom. Email us at www.daleandjena.com. If not, what is holding you back?

Friend, let God take you on a journey to reveal the shame that has held you and your marriage hostage for far too long. Let God heal you so that you can walk in freedom and then share your scars to comfort and encourage another on a similar journey. Tell others that there is hope. Set yourself free from the prison in which sin has held you shackled for so long. Embrace the forgiveness of God. It truly is the most freeing thing you will ever do.

LEARNING TO LOVE

"If I speak in the tongues of men and of angels, but have not love, I am only a resounding gong or a clanging cymbal. If I have the gift of prophecy and can fathom all mysteries and all knowledge, and if I have a faith that can move mountains, but have not love, I am nothing. If I give all I possess to the poor and surrender my body to the flames, but have not love, I gain nothing" (1 Corinthians 13:1–3).

Many marriages have been damaged by the it's-all-about-me attitude. It is an attitude that rules and reigns whenever husbands and wives focus on themselves and their individual needs. Manipulation of the other is almost always the result. When will we learn not to be selfish? When will we learn to think of others more than ourselves? When will we learn to love? These are tough questions and tough areas in our lives over which to gain victory. Yet scripture clearly calls all believers to be selfless, to think of others first, and to love powerfully and passionately. It is here that we do our most effective ministry.

We have said it a thousand times at our conferences and it bears repeating here: your home must be your first place of ministry. As Christians, too many times everything else and everyone else is our ministry field. But within the walls of our homes we have somehow lost this passion. We don't view our marriages as ministry opportunities. Instead we focus on our own selfish wants and needs. Seeking wholeness

> **Your home must be your first place of ministry.**

apart from God, we manipulate each other in alarming ways to get our needs met. I wonder what our lives would look like if our homes were to become our ministry field? What if you learned to love like Christ loved then lived this out in your marriage and homes first? Do you think your marriage would be stronger? Do you think your family would be stronger? Do you think your walk with Christ and your service to him would be more passionate and purposeful?

We do, and that's why in this chapter we are going to focus on 1 Corinthians 13. The love chapter, as it is commonly called, will be our foundational scripture for love and ministry within marriage. Through the guidance of the Holy Spirit, we pray that manipulation and selfishness will be revealed and crucified in your relationship so that your marriage, your home, and your walk with Christ will have passion and power as you follow Him.

Most of the time when we use the word love it is about us and the satisfaction we receive from whatever is the object of our affection. We even approach our walk with Christ like this. If we are not very, very careful, we can make this whole thing about us. 1 John 4:19 reminds us that HE loved us first. Being reminded of this really helps us, especially in marriage, because it's not about us; it's all about HIM.

Love is a strong emotion. It drives our feelings, our flesh, our selfishness. But love is so much more than emotion. It involves commitment, determination, dedication. The entire message and life of Christ is summed up by the commands to love God and to love people (Matthew 22:37–39). In 1 Corinthians 13 God gives us a clear, concise, and detailed description of the agape (unconditional, godly) love husbands and wives should share:

"Love is patient, love is kind and is not jealous; love does not brag and is not arrogant, does not act unbecomingly; it does not seek its own, is not provoked, does not take into account a wrong suffered, does not rejoice in unrighteousness, but rejoices with the truth; bears all things, believes all things, hopes all things, endures all things. Love never fails" (1 Corinthians 13:4–8a NASB).

When Jena and I reflect on our marriage and the baggage we brought into the relationship, is it no wonder we battled instead of ministering. Our road toward authenticity and wholeness has been paved with the conscious decision and commitment to apply the calling of ministry in our marriage.

In marriage you will be constantly faced with what we call "you-or-me" choices. The practical, real-life examples that follow will clearly show how Jena and I manipulated each other. Keep in mind the deep-rooted needs of intimacy and importance along with the backdrop of experience that comes from our family of origin. All these dynamics, our personal propensity for selfishness, and the fact that no one ever explained any of this to us in the first place—much less taught us how to be husbands and wives—led us many times to be manipulators and not ministers in our marriage. The good news is this: you can learn from our mistakes and make a conscious decision to become a minister in your marriage just as we have.

We all entered this world crying, wanting our own way, wanting to be comforted and consoled. We learned from an early age to be manipulators. This is why it is so natural for selfishness and a need for personal satisfaction to be rampant in marriages. After we remarried, our counselor told us, "So many times, I wanted to shake you and tell you to stop acting like kids and grow up." A lack of ministry in marriage will happen when a husband and wife, while they are full-grown adults, act like children in big people's bodies. As you read about our shortcomings, we pray that you will see areas in your life that need to change, and that you will move from a selfish perspective to a ministry perspective.

> **A lack of ministry in marriage will happen when a husband and wife, while they are full-grown adults, act like children in big people's bodies.**

Love Is Patient

The Greek word for patient is *makrothumeo*. It implies forbearance, endurance with mildness and without resentment or indignation. In our home the struggle with patience showed up this way. I hated to be late. To show everybody that I had it all together, I always wanted to be on time to church, but Sundays were often frantic and furious. Jena would scurry about with the regular Sunday morning routine including getting the kids ready for church, and when it was time to go, I would grow impatient and begin yelling, jingling my keys, and honking the car horn. Jena's and my tempers would flare. We would then ride to church in silence, supposedly prepared for ministry and worship.

Impatience was also a problem when our expectations weren't met. Jena had in her mind the kind of spiritual journey I should be on. Many times she criticized me for not praying enough, not reading my Bible enough, or not leading the family the way she thought I should. She was impatient with my spiritual growth. Many a wife's intentions may be good and some of the facts true, but because a man's deep desire is to feel important, the constant sense of failure causes him to retaliate or to quit trying.

Today we are patient with the journey God has for each of us. We work together to get the kids ready for church. We realize that as individuals we don't always approach or handle things the same way and that's okay. We don't nag and demand but we demonstrate long-suffering (mildness, patient endurance). And we love intently by praying for each other.

Love Is Kind

Like yours, our family has taken many trips to Walmart. During one of our recent adventures there, we got out of the car and approached the entrance right behind an elderly woman. When she dropped her keys, I (Dale) immediately bent down and picked them up for her. When I did, she showered me with accolades, compliments, and encouragement. The thank-yous were numerous. I, with swelled head, showed her that chivalry was not dead. As Jena and the kids walked through the store, they noticed how proudly I walked, strutting around after performing such a good deed. When we went to checkout, Jena reached into her purse, pulled out her checkbook, and dropped her keys. As the knight in shining armor by her side, I said, "Hey Jena, you dropped your keys." Where did the kindness go? Why was I so kind to a woman I didn't know but not to Jena? We thought about this later and realized some truths that gave us a new perspective on our marriage. First, Jena expected me to pick up her keys; after all, I had just done it for a stranger. Second, I didn't pick up her keys because I took her for granted, knowing that she was quite capable of picking them up herself. Third, I perceived my ministry field with the wrong perspective. I did not consider my marriage as a place of ministry.

We view our children, our church, our friendships, and even the perfect stranger at Walmart as our ministry field yet God has called us to minister first to our mates. The Bible clearly states in 1 Timothy 3:5 that a man cannot manage the things of God if he cannot manage his own home. The sad truth in marriages today is that we are more patient and kind to perfect strangers and friends than we are to our own mates. When we don't get our needs met, we say and do very unkind things to force our spouses to respond to us. This is neediness and manipulation in its purest form.

But to be kind in marriage is to be gentle in behavior and courteous in heart. It is characterized by outstretched arms and open hands that show favor, blessing, and honor to the mate God has given to us. Now that's ministering

> **To be kind in marriage is to be gentle in behavior and courteous in heart.**

through kindness. Ephesians 4:32 says, *"Be kind and compassionate to one another, forgiving each other, just as in Christ God forgave you."* We asked an elderly couple who attended one of our conferences the secret to their 50-plus years of marriage and they both answered, "We just learned to be kind to each other." Kindness goes a long way in preserving a marriage.

Love Is Content

First Corinthians 13 says love is not jealous. When we looked up the definition, we read words like envious of another's success, resentment for someone's advantage, suspicions or fear of being replaced by a rival. We also found the opposite of jealousy defined as confidence, contentment, and being satisfied. So what about you? Are you confident, content, and satisfied in your marriage? Let us be clear here. If you said no, we are not saying you should get out. What we are saying is that learning to really love in your marriage will require a conscious decision on your part to not compete, to not be envious, and to not let resentment take root in your life and marriage.

So many couples are not content in the relationship simply because they are looking for their spouse to fill a need in their lives that only Christ can fill. They are allowing their unmet needs to lead them to a loss of contentment in the marriage. Listen, we

> **So many couples are simply not content in the relationship because they are looking for their spouse to fill a need in their lives that only Christ can fill!**

understand how powerful unmet needs, a lack of validation, a lack of respect, and a lack security in marriage can be. Remember chapter three, "Empty Hearts, Empty Homes"? This is why we have to understand how these needs drive us. Any time a spouse feels unimportant or that other things have taken precedent over him or her, there is likely to be a struggle with envy and jealousy. Because of this, many husbands and wives find themselves battling to be #1 in the relationship. Secretly they strive to be liked more by their kids. They even manipulate and do things in their marriage and parenting in order to be thought of more highly by their friends. They are rivals, not partners, because they compete and compare what they are doing relative to their spouse. They have a "check-list marriage" that keeps and checks off the things they do right and the things their spouse does wrong. A marriage like this one does not breed contentment.

Our personal standard of living is another area of marriage where we are called to be content. Marriages often struggle because couples compare their lives with the wealth and accomplishments of others. "Keeping up with the Joneses" can drive a wedge between a couple as the pressure rises to acquire more. If we're not careful, we will begin to live outside our means instead of being content with what God has provided. Hebrews 13:5 says to *"keep your lives free from the love of money and be content with what you have, because God has said, 'Never will I leave you; never will I forsake you.'"* It would be a great display of love to clearly communicate to your spouse that your love is unconditional and that you are content with where you are together as Christ continues to grow you. This doesn't mean that you don't strive to improve, but rather you are content while ever striving. The Apostle Paul understood this when he wrote Philippians 4:11–13: *"I am not saying this because I am in need, for I have learned to be content whatever the circumstances. I know what it is to be in need, and I know what it is to have plenty. I have learned the secret of being content in any and every situation, whether well fed or hungry, whether living in plenty or in want. I can do everything through him who gives me strength."* Paul knew that the very strength of Christ in his life was the source of his contentment. If you are going to love like this in your marriage, then Christ must become your strength as well.

Love Is Humble

Love does not brag or vaunt itself; rather it honors and prefers one another (Romans 12:10). Loving through humility requires that you take the position described in Philippians 2—have the same attitude as Christ Jesus. Manipulation shows up when couples in the heat of an argument begin stacking their decks. In the midst of conflict, we operate out of the principle that he who has the most cards in his deck wins! So we stack our decks with such statements as *I always do [this and this and this] . . . and you don't do anything.* The stacking language of "I always" and "You never" builds us up to a higher position, somehow gaining what we perceive to be leverage in the battle. The reality is that this is all about you bragging on yourself and not you humbly loving your mate. To be humble does not mean that you think less of yourself; being humble means you think of yourself less. In other words, the marriage is not always about you and what you can get from it. Authentic love in a marriage always requires humility because it is the essence of Christ. Jesus, speaking of himself in Matthew 11:29, said, *"Take my yoke upon you and learn from me, for I am gentle and humble in heart, and you will find rest for your souls."* Psalm 18:27 reminds us: *"You save the humble but bring low those whose eyes are haughty."* Do you want to elevate your marriage and bring peace and rest to your soul? Then learn to love through humility. After all, it is the humble whom the Lord guides, teaches, and leads in His ways (Psalm 25:9)

> **Authentic love in marriage always requires humility because it is the essence of Christ.**

Love Is Not Arrogant

This quality of love carries humility much deeper. While we are to be humble and to not brag, criticism through arrogance carries with it a completely different set of problems. The action here consists of pride and conceit. Pride cometh before a fall, and God says that He hates it. We attempt to control our spouses emotionally with pride, arrogance, and conceit, and by thinking we know it all. We think we are right all the time and often shame our spouse into feelings of worthlessness. We are too proud to say we are sorry even when we know we are wrong. We are too conceited to admit that we have hurt each other so we stonewall, pout, and give the cold shoulder instead of loving. Arrogance stems from an attitude that we know the minds, actions, and motives of our spouses. We make statements such as *They've always been that way, and they always will be; there's no changing them.* Husbands and wives should strive not to be puffed up but modest, allowing change to occur by the Spirit of God working in their spouse—understanding that it is God's job to change their spouse, not theirs. Loving husbands and wives pray for their spouses and demonstrate godly characteristics in their own lives that will demonstrate to their mates the very qualities of Christ. This kind of love says *I will not be conceited or demand my own way.* Loving your spouse without arrogance is God's command.

Love Is Decent, Moral, and Mannerly

Love does not behave in an unbecoming or unseemly way. The Greek word *aschemoneo* used in 1 Corinthians 13:5 speaks of defying a moral and mannerly standard. Love is not rude or ill-mannered. During the early years of our marriage, I loved to tell jokes at Jena's expense. While you may not think of that as indecent, the reality is that it was dishonoring and rude behavior toward her. The root of the issue was my need to feel important. When my friends laughed and thought I was funny, I felt important. But it was not loving to treat her with disrespect. We have had many couples, men and women alike, who have shared with us that their spouse makes them feel stupid and minimizes their feelings instead of validating them. Decent, moral, and mannerly love carries with it common courtesy. Often when we have guests in our home, the pleases, thank-yous, and compliments fill the air. Yet when we are at home alone, we suddenly treat each other with an entirely different set of rules. In other words, we are not using our manners. Loving each other in the marriage relationship means you should never be embarrassing, unbecoming, or unseemly at the expense of your mate.

Loving requires respecting each other and choosing to hold your spouse in high regard before others.

Love Is Unselfish

The selfish heart is at the core of all marital struggles. Read that sentence again. The selfish heart is at the core of all marital struggles. If it were not for selfishness, the divorce rate in this country would be basically non-existent. Selfishness drives all of us. Isaiah 53:6 says, *"We all, like sheep, have gone astray, each of us has turned to his own way."* Let's face it, because of our sin nature, every one of us is selfish to the core. Praise God, He has given us new life through Christ: *"The old has gone, the new has come!"* (2 Corinthians 5:17). We are to put off the old and put on the new, being transformed into Christ's image, becoming more like Him and less like us. The absolute best way to do this is to follow the command of God and to love our spouses as ourselves (Matthew 22:39). But here's the problem. Because we are selfish, we tend to love ourselves more than we do our spouses. We disobey God because we'd rather have our own needs met. We want our way on our timetable. Unselfish love, however, commands that we constantly ask *How can I serve my spouse today?* This does not mean that you become a doormat or that everything is one-sided. It does not mean you get taken advantage of. It does mean however, that you become a giver more than a taker. If both spouses would learn to love from a giver perspective rather than a taker perspective, love would transform their homes.

> **If both spouses would learn to love from a giver perspective rather than a taker perspective, love would transform their home.**

Love Is Even-Tempered

Anger, hot-temperedness, being easily provoked, being irritating, and threatening are all forms of control in marriage. Yet 1 Corinthians commands that we demonstrate our love by being even-tempered. Being angry and hot-tempered is a serious problem in marriages today. At the heart of anger is hurt. Our neediness and expectations are unfulfilled, so we vent. Our spouse has done or said something that hurt us, so we lash out in anger. In our marriage, it showed up like this: Jena would have a deep need to be encouraged emotionally. She would want me to verbally affirm her—to tell her how much I love her and encourage her in her walk with the Lord. Yet when I didn't, or didn't in the way Jena expected, she would become demanding. Because I (like most people) don't like to fail, I would respond in anger hoping that Jena would stop being so demanding. I thought my apparent anger would stop Jena from criticizing. Our intimacy was broken down by our demanding spirits, controlling attitudes, and anger. This is not God's plan for loving each other. Loving your spouse as described in 1 Corinthians 13 means that you make decisions that soften and do not irritate your husband or wife. You demonstrate love to your spouse in a manner that stimulates positive responses and calming attitudes.

Love Is Forgiving

We'll discuss authentic forgiveness thoroughly in a later chapter, but for our discussion in this chapter we need to point out that learning to love is demonstrated through true, God-like forgiveness. Very simply, love does not keep a record of wrongs. We remember many arguments from the early days of our marriage when in the heat of battle one or both of us would bring up something that happened months or even years before. We would be right in the middle of a disagreement and Jena would say, "I remember in 1984 when you said that my hair looked stupid!" I would respond, "Well, I remember in 1984 when you forgot my birthday present!" We keep these records of wrongs, or our ledger of debits and credits, just in case we might need them in the future. The fact is, most of us cash in our credits and keep the debits as a weapon to use later. Bringing up past hurt and pain when these should have been forgiven is not love. The motive behind our behavior is that we want our spouse to hurt as much as he or she has hurt us. This is a vengeful attitude and one of the most unloving things you can do in a marriage. Love is when you and your spouse understand the degree of forgiveness you have received from Christ and through ministry to each other, you offer that same degree of forgiveness.

Love Is Righteous

Love does right by others. It doesn't seek to hurt them physically, mentally, spiritually, or emotionally. Our love for our spouses should be so rich and genuine that it is righteous by its very nature. So what is righteousness? Simply put, it is to be right with God. It means you are thinking, feeling, acting, and living your life wholly conformed to the Word of God and the ways of God. We know this is a challenge because the Bible says that no one is righteous, no not one, and that all have sinned and fallen short of the glory of God (Romans 3:10). Praise God that while we were sinners, Christ died for us.

It is this gift of Christ that makes us righteous. When we accept Him, we are placed into a position of righteousness. We then will desire to live up to that position. In other words, we will want our walk to match our talk. In marriage, the way we love and treat each other shows that we are right with God. Plainly stated, when we demonstrate the character of Christ through righteous love, we are committed to loving each other the way Christ loves us.

Love Is Truthful

Marital breakdown occurs in a marriage when deceit and dishonesty rule. It would occur in our marriage whenever we would have conversations about upcoming events or plans for the weekend and I would tell Jena only the "necessary" information. For example, one Thursday night we were sitting in the den talking about what we would be doing that weekend. I knew I had a tee time on the golf course on Sunday afternoon but had failed to mention it to Jena. Instead we made plans for what we would do together on Saturday. Saturday night I said, "Oh, Jena, by the way, I have a tee time tomorrow at 1:30." Jena responded, "We've been together all day. Why are you just now mentioning this? Why didn't you tell me about this Thursday night when we were discussing plans for the weekend? What else are you not telling me?" Trust started to break down between us. It would also happen whenever Jena knew she wanted to have a night out with the girls. As we would discuss our plans, the night out would be downplayed: "By the way, some girls and I are gonna go to the movies tonight. You don't mind, do you?" Jena would have known for days the plans for this girls night out but would fail to be completely truthful because she didn't want me to object. Many couples communicate with the attitude of what they don't know won't hurt them or I'll tell my spouse on a 'need to know basis.' Truthful love in marriage compels us to be honest and forthright. Love rejoices in the truth. This truth is so much more, however, than just sharing facts and plans. Loving through truth is about character as you demonstrate a lifestyle of truth and honesty in your marriage. Loving truth rejoices whenever you as a couple are grounded in the application and expression of God's truth and

> **Loving truth rejoices when you as a couple are grounded in the application and expression of God's truth and His Word in your life.**

His Word in your life. Loving truth is powerful in marriage when we allow God's Word to conquer and overcome our sinful nature. When we walk in obedience to God's Word, our lives and our marriages are conformed into accurate representations of His truth living in our hearts and homes.

Truthful love in marriage understands that without truth, trust is lost.

Love Bears All Things

The Greek word *stego*, used in 1 Corinthians 13:7, means to cover as a roof or to patiently endure; to put up with. When a storm comes, you naturally head for cover. You patiently endure the rain under some form of shelter until the rain subsides. So it is with marriage. The struggles and stresses of life are going to come like a storm approaching your home. Rather than running to the quickest way out, God desires for us to patiently endure while running together under His umbrella of protection until the struggles subside. God-like love bears all things. Learning to endure, or to put up with, each other's weaknesses creates marriage partners of grace. This does not mean we settle for second best; it simply means we are to love in such a way that we bear all things with each other, bestow grace to each other, and allow our mate to grow and change into the person Christ wants him or her to become. Growing, godly couples love each other by bearing all things and weathering the storms of life.

Love Believes All Things

Our fleshly nature and selfish attitudes often cause us to be skeptics—untrusting of others. Of course this occurs because many marriages live in past hurt instead of present hope. We hang onto moments of past failures and disappointments. Jena and I remember vividly in our marriage—especially in the days of our heated battles and arguments—how we believed the negative about each other rather than the positive. In the middle of our divorce proceedings, it was very common for Jena to make statements such as, "I've heard it all before. Your words mean nothing to me. You can't give me one good reason to stay married to you!" I responded, "You talk a good game, but I don't believe a word you say." These cutting, critical statements would drive a wedge deeply between us. Yet love in marriage should believe all things. You choose to believe the best of your spouse, trusting until you're given a reason not to. It means the direction of your will is to seek the positive rather than the negative. It means that you love each other by looking for the best, seeking ways to encourage and exhort. It is a conscious decision to love by hoping for the best while giving the benefit of the doubt.

Love Hopes All Things

Hope in love is powerful! Many couples today are struggling because they feel their marriage is hopeless. We certainly did. Yet we know from firsthand experience that there is always hope with Jesus. He is the giver of hope and is capable of restoring the most hopeless relationship. We remember the day we started our journey toward authenticity. We asked ourselves, *Is this possible? Can we do this? Is this hopeless?* As we journeyed through the uncharted waters, it was our hope in Christ that carried us through. As Christ continued to reveal Himself as faithful and true, our hope in each other through Christ began to take on an entirely new focus. As Christ began to change us, we moved from a hopeless situation to a hope-filled relationship. When we approached our reconciliation with the power of having hope in Jesus and then each other, Christ restored all the love and so much more that had been lost. The bottom line: it was a faith moment for us. Did we truly believe in the power of God to restore and renew? Could we lay down our selfish, hopeless perspectives and live out the principle that the love of Christ hopes for all things? *"Now these three remain: faith, hope and love. But the greatest of these is love" (1 Corinthians 13:13).* As faith in God strengthens, hope showers down. It is this hope—the hope of glory—that catapults us to God-like love.

Love Endures All Things

In 1 Corinthians 13:7, the Greek word for endure, *hupomeno*, means to remain, to have fortitude, and to persevere. You may be facing the most difficult time in your marriage. You may have reared your children and now find that your marriage is empty because your house is empty. You may have been let down, hurt, disappointed, betrayed, and facing many trials and troubles. There were many days for Jena and me that our flesh cried out for us to walk away, give up, and quit. Since our divorce and remarriage, we have realized how weak our love really was. Oh, friend, walking away and quitting is not the answer. We want to impress upon you to stand your ground and endure because of Christ's love for you. Enduring love says that regardless of the response or lack of response, whether rejecting or embracing the actions and attitudes of my spouse, I am going to behave with integrity and in the right manner. It means that I am responsible for making sure my behavior is godly. Sometimes my spouse is not lovable, but I am going to endure and love her anyway. Sometimes he rejects me and remains distant, but I am going to continue to pursue and love him. Sometimes my spouse simply won't receive my actions and attempts, yet I understand that enduring love is more about giving than receiving. In fact, I am doing the right thing out of obedience to Christ— because of my love for Him. Remember: Christ's love for you endured all the way to the cross. Therefore, you are called to live a life of enduring love, understanding that this kind of love changes

> **You are called to live a life of enduring love, understanding that this kind of love changes hearts and lives.**

hearts and lives. However, let us be clear that enduring love does not mean you allow abusive situations to continue. Sin carries consequences, and love never helps someone sin. The highest level of enduring love would be to set appropriate boundaries and get help for you and your spouse so that godly, Christ-like love can be developed.

Love Never Fails

Do you really believe that love never fails? Are you so consumed by your own needs and fears that you are afraid your love will fail? Is your marriage failing? Is your relationship with your spouse empty and bankrupt? Is it even possible that your love for each other can return? All of these are questions that we faced. Our hearts' desire is to communicate that a godly marriage is available to each and every one of you. We know that applying the principles of 1 Corinthians 13 works. It teaches us to love the way God intended. That kind of love never fails. His Word is true; you can count on it. But will you choose to love regardless? It is a matter of obedience to His Word that enables you to find yourself on the ministry side of love. As we conclude, take another moment to look at the scripture: *"Love is patient, love is kind. It does not envy, it does not boast, it is not proud. It is not rude, it is not self-seeking, it is not easily angered, it keeps no record of wrongs. Love does not delight in evil but rejoices with the truth. It always protects, always trusts, always hopes, always perseveres. Love never fails."*

Where do you find yourself as you are learning to love? Are you demonstrating the sixteen qualities of agape love to your mate? Can you replace the word "love" with your name in the Scripture? This is to be our goal. When you learn to love like this, you will be both truly and biblically loving your mate. Will you dedicate yourself to loving your spouse the way 1 Corinthians 13 commands? We hope so, because it is the way we found (and you will find) authenticity and wholeness in marriage.

OWN YOUR STUFF

"As iron sharpens iron, so one man sharpens another" (Proverbs 27:17).

We are more than halfway through our journey together! It has been our sincere prayer that you and your marriage have experienced newfound freedom, purpose, and passion as you GET REAL with the Lord and each other. Hopefully, you see how deliberate we have been on our journey together. We pray you have taken off some masks as you have learned how to hold each other's hearts well, to find your needs totally fulfilled in Christ, and to fight the enemy well while being delivered from strongholds and shame. Wow, what a journey! This chapter is a critical one. It's critical because some couples would rather skip this chapter or pass the buck, so they mentally and emotionally check out. We hope that's not you! Hang on. There is much more the Lord wants to do in your life and your marriage. We truly believe the Lord is going to faithfully complete the good work He started in us as we remain steadfast in Him (Philippians 1:6).

It's also a critical week because every couple we know has faced, is facing, or will face where we are headed this week. From the engaged couple to the empty-nester, none of us are exempt; we all deal with the challenge of this week's journey. In one simple word, we are talking about CONFLICT. The longer we live, the more we are convinced that conflict is going to happen in every relationship. It's happening in marriages; it's happening in the lives of our kids; it's happening at work, with neighbors, and with people in our small groups and churches. Yes, conflict is a given! In fact, we bet you could write down right now one or two conflicts in your marriage that you wish were resolved!

Based on Proverbs 27:17, ask yourself this question: How could this conflict make me sharper spiritually and relationally? In other words, what is God after in the midst of conflict? You see, until we learn to look at our conflicts the way Christ looks at our conflicts, we are going to make a mess of our relationships. In fact, we should ask this question about everything we face in life. There is so much freedom, purpose, and transformation when we are able to see everything that happens in our lives as divine opportunities for Christ to grow us, shape us, and form us into His image. That is exactly why we must learn to handle conflict with a Christ-like view and in a Christ-like manner.

> **Until we learn to look at our conflicts the way Christ looks at our conflicts, we are going to make a mess of our relationships.**

CHOICES IN THE MIDST OF CONFLICT

Have you ever noticed that we live in a world where choices are innumerable? Just walk into a local bookstore and see all the books from which to choose; go to a local restaurant and choose from the wide variety of menu items; take a trip to your local department store, walk down the aisles, and see the countless choices of clothes, accessories, toys, and gadgets. From ice cream flavors to the latest fashions, our world is filled with choices. Conflict is no different; it too comes with a set of choices. Which one do you most often make?

Choosing to Retreat and Avoid

The first choice we have in the midst of conflict is to retreat. There are many of us who simply do not like conflict. We will do whatever we have to do to avoid it. As soon as tension and stress gets in the marriage, many men and women alike will quickly withdraw, shut down, and isolate themselves. Listen, we understand. In the midst of the battle, when feelings are raw, you are wounded, and emotions are high, it is so easy to retreat. In fact, sometimes that is a good choice (for a brief moment) as long as you set a time later to work through the conflict. Sometimes you need a "cooling off" period. It is better to walk away for a moment and let things settle than to continue the conflict in an ungodly and unholy way. No one has ever had to apologize for an unkind word never spoken. Cooling off, being a person of self-control, considerate of your spouse's feelings, and knowing your relational weak points so that you don't wound each other, are all good things.

The problem comes when there is total avoidance and you never work through the issue at hand. We are talking about the "continual retreater" who disengages in the relationship and avoids conflict at all cost. People who are "continual retreaters" never resolve the conflict, they never grow, and the marriage never gets transformed. Most of the time it is because they refuse to look at themselves and to stay engaged in the relationship, allowing Christ to use it as a moment of transformation and refinement. Over time the "continual retreater" usually turns into a "stuffer." He just stuffs all of his emotions and never lets his spouse know of the problems. When all the dust settles and life gets back to some sense of normalcy, the conflict is still there, as unresolved as it ever was. Sadly, years of continually stuffing the hurt, anger, and frustration into the depths of his soul has now turned into bitterness. Sooner or later the unresolved conflict and bitterness turns into anger. Much like a shaken Dr. Pepper, one incident, whether small or large, can "pop the cap" of one's heart, and soon he or she will spew angry words like daggers to the heart of his or her spouse. Because the "continual retreater" turned into a stuffer and avoided the conflict, their bitterness and anger spews forth doing serious damage.

When we think about retreating, the first Bible story that comes to mind is the story of Jonah. God told Jonah to head to Nineveh to speak on His behalf (Jonah 1:2), yet he chose to run away to Tarshish. There were several reasons why he retreated, but in the midst of all of these, we believe fear played a major part. Fear can be an enormous motivator.

Perhaps instead of retreating in fear, avoiding conflict at all cost, the most loving thing you could do is to push through your fear and talk through things with your spouse. 1 John 4:18 says, *"There is no fear in love. But perfect love drives out fear, because fear has to do with punishment. The one who fears is not made perfect in love."* May you begin to truly know God's depth of love for you so that you will have the confidence to work through your conflicts instead of avoiding them.

Choosing to Rebel

Some people are not "continual retreaters"; they are "continual rebellers." So, if you are not one who retreats, you might be one who rebels. The word rebellion means what you think it does: defiant, stubborn, obstinate, stiff-necked, and disobedient. "Continual rebellers" are people who always have to be right, always have to have the last word, and rarely admit they are wrong. Consequently, they have a hard time owning their stuff. They just can't seem to say they are wrrrrr…ong!

So why do we rebel? Why do we feel the need to dig in our heels and come out fighting? Isaiah 53:6 says we each want our own way. The world we live in, with its Burger King "have-it-your-way" mentality, promotes this desire. Ephesians 4:22 and James 4:1-2 reminds us that there is a battle that wages within our souls because we have insatiable desires. Simply put, if not careful, we will do whatever we have to do to get our own way.

Because this is so deeply ingrained in our flesh, we choose to rebel because we want to be right. Just like "continual retreaters", "continual rebellers" don't want to admit that they are wrong. They come out fighting, deflecting, and blaming others for their behavior with words like, *Well, I would never have done [this] if you hadn't done [that]! I would have never said what I said if you hadn't said what you said. You made me say that!* The problem with these statements is that it causes one person to take all of the blame while the rebeller is never held responsible for the part that he or she played. Rebellers never have the conviction or see the need for change in their behavior so conflict and pain continues in the relationship. They remain the same in their ungodly behavior because they have passed off responsibility to another by rationalizing and justifying their actions.

Here's the challenge: Within all of us is a rebellious nature that wants its own way. That's why we are convinced of this one truth: Our problem is not that we don't know what to do but that we are unwilling to do it! Too many times—especially in the midst of conflict—we make a selfish choice rather than a selfless one. The Word of God speaks about the heart condition and the consequences of rebellion. Read the following passages and ask the Lord to reveal to you where you might struggle with rebellion.

Proverbs 29:1 says, *"A man who remains stiff-necked after many rebukes will suddenly be destroyed—without remedy."* This is the result of continual rebellion. Yet God is calling us to live on a higher plane, rising above the fleshly tendencies that so strongly drive us. In the midst of conflict—when emotions and feelings are raw—if you choose your own sinful way and rebel, you will have a hard time listening to your spouse. When you rebel, destruction

> **In the midst of conflict—when emotions and feelings are raw—if you choose your own sinful way and rebel, you will have a hard time listening to your spouse. When you rebel, destruction of the relationship is inevitable!**

of the relationship is inevitable! Wow, how easy it is for this to happen. We can remember so many arguments where we walked down that very path. Our conflicts were full of pride, selfishness, and stubbornness, driving us to the point of not even being able to listen to each other. Just like it is so easy to retreat, it is so easy to rebel! That's why we said earlier that we must learn to handle conflict with a Christ-like view and in a Christ-like manner.

> **We must learn to handle conflict with a Christ-like view and in a Christ-like manner.**

Owning Your Stuff – Choosing Responsibility

Usually a marriage has one "continual retreater" and one "continual rebeller." If they never see themselves or conflict as an "iron sharpening iron" opportunity for transformation and growth, they will have a marriage less than fulfilling and free. But if a couple can view conflict as an opportunity to grow into the image of Christ, they will choose to lay down their selfishness, fear, and pride, and make the God-honoring choice of owning their stuff. Friends, in the midst of conflict, if you want to live on a higher plane as a couple—if you want a genuine, grace-filled relationship—you must choose to take responsibility for your actions.

Like many of you, we learn so much about ourselves by watching our kids. We remember a specific time when our kids were little and got into an argument. Our daughter Jorja was around four years old, sitting on the floor watching television. Cole, our seven-year-old son, came into the room and with total disregard for Jorja, what she was doing, or her feelings, changed the channel (Sounds like some adults we know). Anyway, you need to know that Cole was constantly picking at Jorja, tripping her, bossing her around because he thought that's what big brothers could do, or at least get away with (Sounds like some other adults we know). He had also been fully warned by both of us that one day Jorja would grow up and would get him, and we were going to let her! Well, that day came as we heard a blood-curdling scream from our den. Turning the corner from the kitchen, we discovered Jorja, in a full-on death grip, grabbing Cole by the hair. She was pulling it so tightly that he was screaming at the top of his lungs. The moment she saw us, her face went from a teeth gritting growl to a full-fledged grin! After countless "we-told-you-so's", Jena proceeded to take Cole and Jorja over to the sofa to discuss what had happened. When she asked Cole what he did, his response was, "Mommy, Mommy, she pulled my hair!" Jena said, "Cole, I didn't ask you what Jorja did; I asked you what you did." He said, "Mom, big boys don't watch kiddie shows, so I changed the channel." When Jorja was asked about the part she played in the conflict, her answer was much the same: "Mommy, Cole changed the channel. He changed the channel!" Doesn't that sound just like some married couple entrenched in a conflict? We are just little kids in big people bodies! Blaming, shaming, and passing the buck, refusing to own our stuff while trying to get the speck out of our brother's eye, blinded by the beam in our own (Matthew 7:3). Way too many spouses are blaming the other for their behavior, rarely admitting their part of the conflict. At that moment, Jena began to discuss with Cole and Jorja their choices, their selfishness, their wanting their own way, and ultimately their SIN. She then asked Cole and Jorja to do a few things. She asked them to confess their sin, call it sin, and seek the other's forgiveness. Jorja was required to say, "Cole, I pulled your hair and it was wrong. It was sin. I am sorry. Will you forgive me?" And Cole had to do the same. As soon as we sent them off, the Spirit of God convicted us both. We were instantly reminded that we just asked our kids to do something we rarely do! Wow, talk about conviction. If you are going to bring wholeness to your marriage, you are going to have to start

> **If you are going to bring wholeness to your marriage, you are going to have to start owning your stuff.**

owning your stuff. Oh, what our marriages, homes, churches, communities, and world would look like if we would just stop rationalizing our choices, retreating, and rebelling in our actions, and call sin what it really is. If couples could just let this principle melt into their hearts, we believe their marital conflicts would dramatically change.

As you think back on your conflicts in marriage, we want to challenge you to do what we asked our kids to do: simply take responsibility to "own your stuff." Before we show you what it takes to own your stuff, take a moment right now and ask the Lord to search your heart. Psalm 4:4 says, *"In your anger do not sin; when you are on your beds, search your hearts and be silent."* Psalm 139:23–24 says, *"Search me, O God, and know my heart; test me and know my anxious thoughts. See if there is any offensive way in me, and lead me in the way everlasting."* Chances are, you are either in the midst of a conflict or just coming out of one. For sure, there will be some in your future. Be silent before the Lord and ask Him to reveal any sin you need to own.

What It Takes to Own Your Stuff

After we were remarried, we went on a journey for months, evaluating what happened in the breakdown of our marriage. Much of what you are going through in this study is the result of our journey toward authenticity and wholeness. If anyone had ever made wrong choices in the midst of conflict, we were definitely that couple. During the first eight years of our first marriage, we had way too much retreating and rebelling and very little owning of our stuff. In the last half of this chapter, we want to invite you to walk the pathway we walked to finding what it takes to own your stuff. We are going to look at three things that are critical to owning your stuff and handling conflict well. They are: God's **destiny** for you, God's **desire** for you, and God's **design** for you!

GOD'S DESTINY FOR YOU

As we have already stated (but it bears repeating), until we learn to look at our conflicts the way Christ looks at our conflicts, we are going to make a mess of our relationships. To really understand this statement, you are going to have to fully understand God's destiny for your life. Only then will you learn to look at your life the way Christ looks at it. According to Ephesians 1:4, Ephesians 4:24, 2 Corinthians 7:1 and 1 Peter 1:13–16, God's chosen destiny for you is holiness.

Because we oftentimes have misconceptions of holiness, we are kept from living the abundant, passion-filled, purpose-driven life of a Christian. Too many Christians have boiled down their faith experience to keeping the rules with a "God-is-good-you-are-bad-now-stop-it" approach to Christianity. Friend, God has so much more in store for you than your merely managing your sin well. He has an abundant, exciting, joy-filled faith walk for you, with your destiny being holiness.

Do you believe that God knows what is best for you? Do you really believe that He wants the very best for you? If you said yes to both of these, then perhaps you should exchange some of your misconceptions and wrong approaches to holiness. So what is holiness? There is no way in this chapter to fully explain everything that is encompassed in this word. But simply stated, to be HOLY means to be set apart unto God. In other words, you are totally God's. Just as I (Dale) am totally Jena's, I am totally God's. Because I am Jena's, I no longer date others, and I realize that all of my decisions affect her. She carries my name so I am committed to her and her alone. As one that is wholly God's, I no longer "date" the world, and I am conscious that my decisions affect the name of Christ which I carry. To be sure, holiness is more about your character than your behavior. It is the very nature of God (for He is holy) being reproduced in your heart. Holiness is what emanates from God. It is His essence. And because it is His essence, it needs also to be ours. Holiness is a process of striving to be more like Christ.

What if you really embraced the fact that Christ died so that you could be holy? Would your choices and character look different if it was based on the truth that "in Him you live and move and have your being?" What would your marriage look like if you simply renewed yourself inwardly, day by day, as you went through life? Would things change if you really did everything in Christ's name because you were striving to be holy in all that you do, being set apart by truth? Do you think your conflict would look different if you would imitate Christ in the midst of it? Perhaps you, like so many couples, have a difficult time seeing Christ in your conflicts because you have simply lost your pursuit of holiness. Do you want a radical, biblical approach to owning your stuff? Then pursue holiness in the midst of the conflict. After all, Hebrews 12:14 reminds us: *"without holiness, no one will see the Lord!"*

GOD'S DESIRE FOR YOU

The reason God's destiny for you is holiness is because He has an incredible desire for you. So what is it? INTIMACY! Let that sink in. INTIMACY! The creator of the universe, our Holy, righteous, and loving Heavenly Father desires intimacy with you. In his book, *Gripped by the Greatness of God*, James MacDonald writes:

> "God displays holiness as the central and defining essence of His character. I know that some people think that God is defined by love, but I would beg to differ. If love was at the very center of God's nature, then He could have welcomed us into heaven without the atoning death of His Son Jesus. Fact is, God's holiness demanded that sin be paid for, and then His love compelled Him to pay the price Himself."

Do you see this? Because of God's holiness, His love compelled Him to have Jesus die for us so that we could be redeemed and restored (1 Peter 1:18–23). God desires a face-to-face, intimate relationship with you. Christ even prayed this for you. John 17:20–23 says, *"My prayer is not for them alone. I pray also for those who will believe in me through their message, that all of them may be one, Father, just as you are in me and I am in you. May they also be in us so that the world may believe that you have sent me. I have given them the glory that you gave me, that they may be one as we are one: I in them and you in me. May they be brought to complete unity to let the world know that you sent me and have loved them even as you have loved me."*

Christ is praying for us to be intimate with Him with the same intimacy He had with His Father. Here's the bottom line: without the pursuit of holiness and without embracing God's desire for intimacy, we will not experience the abundant life our Heavenly Father so painfully provided.

We also believe that Christ prayed this powerful prayer for you because He knows that intimacy with Christ creates intimacy in your marriage. Remember, intimacy is "into me, I will let you see." It is about letting Christ into every area of your life. It is about transparency, no more masks, no more games, no more hiding. Intimacy in marriage is the same thing. It is about openness, transparency, and oneness (Genesis 2:24; John 17:22). Intimacy flees in the face of choosing to retreat and rebel. Make

> **Intimacy flees in the face of choosing to retreat and rebel.**

no mistake about it: there is a direct relationship between our intimate relationship with Christ and our intimate relationship with one another. That's why holiness is God's destiny, and intimacy is His desire.

GOD'S DESIGN FOR YOU

Years ago we went on a quest to find our IDENTITY in Christ. What we found was a new freedom and power for our Christian walk. God's design—who He says we are—is incredibly liberating. No longer were we going to be the "rule-keeping", "performance-based" Christian couple. You see, "rule-keeping", "performance-based" couples are only as good as their latest performance. As long as they perform well or don't break the rules, they are good. But the moment they mess up (and they will), everything changes. Years of this, and the marriage can become very fragile. The couple usually swings from one extreme of perform, perform, perform for approval to the other extreme of just quitting altogether. This is why couples say, "I try and I try and I try, and it's never good enough!"

When a man and woman find out who Christ says they are and they begin living in that design, their lives and marriages change. Jena's Bible study, *Authentic Woman...In Search of the Genuine Article*, was written just for women to help them find out this very thing. We will not have an identity problem when we see ourselves the way God sees us.

God's design for you is pasted throughout the Scriptures. One day, just take some time to read these Scriptures: Genesis 1:27, John 15:15, Romans 8:29, Romans 8:37, Galatians 4:6–7, Ephesians 1:4, Ephesians 2:10, Ephesians 4:23–24, and Colossians 2:9–10. These scriptures are by no means exhaustive. The entire Word of God is full of scriptures about who God says you are. But how comforting to be reminded that you were made in His image and predestined (pre = before, destined = destiny) to be conformed to the likeness of Christ. The very God of the universe calls you His friend and He calls you a conqueror! Not only are you a friend, but a son and an heir. Christ died so that you would be holy and blameless in His sight, created to do good works which He prepared in advance for you to do. The more you walk in this identity, the more you begin to change your attitude about WHO YOU ARE. Then, the more you are compelled to exchange your old ways for new ones because you realize that you were created to be like Christ in true righteousness and holiness. For in Christ all the fullness of the divine nature exists, and you have been given fullness in Christ.

God's destiny is holiness,
    His desire is intimacy, and
        His design for you is Christlikeness.

Friends, in the midst of conflict it is definitely a challenge to own your stuff. As we stated at the beginning of this chapter, it is much easier to retreat or rebel. But God has a bigger plan. We hope you see that now. Yes, even in the midst of conflict—and probably especially through conflict—God wants to perfect you. He wants you to handle conflict differently. He wants you to be set apart in your thinking, feeling, and acting because His destiny for you is HOLINESS. When we don't pursue holiness in our conflicts, we simply will not see Christ in our homes. Remember, our selfish desires, wanting our own way, is at the root of all our relationship discord. Selfishness is destroying marriages at a rampant rate. But praise God, He came shining through with an amazing plan. It is His ultimate plan for everyone on the face of this earth to trust Him with their lives. From the moment of salvation, He is after the recreating of Himself in people.

> **When we don't pursue holiness in our conflicts, we simply will not see Christ in our homes.**

He is after the creation of true holiness and true righteousness in your life. He wants you to partner with the Holy Spirit, allowing Him to do the deep work of ridding you of anything that contaminates and corrupts His presence in your life. We believe that God does this—His deepest, transforming work—in the marriage relationship. We also believe God does His deepest work in the midst of trials, stress, struggles, and conflicts. No wonder marriage is so hard. No wonder conflict in marriage is so critical. No wonder we need to see our conflicts the way Christ sees them. After all, He is after so much more than just the fixing of our problems, He is after the formation of His character in our souls (Galatians 4:19).

LET IT GO

"A man's wisdom gives him patience; it is to his glory to overlook an offense" (Proverbs 19:11).

As we just learned in the last chapter, conflict, if mishandled, can cause a lot of damage in our relationships. You might be suffering the consequences now of conflict that wasn't handled in a godly manner. Don't despair. There is hope. There is a solution. It's called forgiveness. In this chapter, we'll focus on letting it go through authentic forgiveness. We will look at what forgiveness requires and what it looks like in a marriage (or any relationship, for that matter!). Let's face it, forgiveness is hard, and many people have a misconception of what true forgiveness really is and really requires. They have bought into what the world says about forgiveness instead of what God says; believe us, they are vastly different.

Even though we were both saved at an early age, it was not until we experienced our divorce and remarriage that we understood how deeply we had been forgiven—not forgiven by each other necessarily, but forgiven first by Christ. If you are not a believer and you have never accepted the forgiveness of Christ for your sins, then you will never be able to truly forgive others. Your first step toward letting it go and finding true authentic forgiveness must start with your accepting of the grace and goodness of God. All you have to do is ask Christ to come in and save you. He will make you a new creature, born again, to the glory of God. If you have never accepted Christ as your Lord and

Savior, settle the issue right now by turning to the Appendix at the back of this book.

What Forgiveness is NOT (Our Misconceptions)

Before we discuss what true forgiveness is, let us first look intently what forgiveness is not because some of our misconceptions are destroying our marriages. First of all, forgiveness is not forgetting! We have talked to countless couples who walked through forgiveness believing they should be able to forgive and forget. Yes, scripture clearly says in Isaiah 43:25: *"I, even I, am He who blots out your transgressions, for My own sake, and remembers your sins no more."*

Forgiveness is not forgetting!

God, through His awesome mercy and grace, forgives us of our transgressions. And praise God, He remembers them no more. Remember, we are finite-minded people, not all-powerful, infinite gods. We also have an enemy who accuses the brethren both day and night (Revelation 12:10). No wonder then, when a conflict or argument arises, the first thing your enemy wants to do is to stir your memory and bring up the past. Frustrated, you think you can never get through all your stuff because you keep remembering all the hurts and pain you caused and felt. You even wonder if you have forgiven the other person or been forgiven yourself. As people with limitations, we do not always have the ability to forget. We do, however, have the ability to choose how we will respond when confronted with the memory of a past hurt, pain, or sin. Forgiveness is not forgetting, but forgiveness does involve a choice. You can choose what you do with the memory. You can choose not to allow the enemy to keep you hostage to the things you can't forget. So much of the battle is in the battlefield of the mind and is a decision of your will. Philippians 4:8–9 states: *"Finally, brothers, whatever is true, whatever is noble, whatever is right, whatever is pure, whatever is lovely, whatever is admirable—if anything is excellent or praiseworthy—think about such things. Whatever you have learned or received or heard from me, or seen in me—put it into practice. And the God of peace will be with you."*

Did you see this?—*"Think of these things and then put them into practice."* When you do, *"the God of peace will be with you."* Replacing painful memories with the power of God's Word will provide great strength as you demonstrate forgiveness to those who need it. God can transform your mind as you fill it with the truths of His Word. But not only is forgiveness not forgetting; forgiveness is not automatic reconciliation. Many have been taught that after we say I'm sorry, everything should go back to the way it was. The problem is that often we shouldn't want things to go back to the way they were. We want change to take place, as each person recognizes and repents of his sin. Acts 26:20 provides the biblical definition of repentance and reconciliation. The Word of God says: *"...repent and turn to God and prove their repentance by their deeds."*

> **Forgiveness is not automatic reconciliation.**

As you found out in the last chapter, coming through conflict in a God-honoring way can truly transform couples for the better. But this transformation process is just that—a process that takes time and partnership with the Holy Spirit. That is why forgiveness is not automatic reconciliation. It only takes one person to forgive but it takes two people to reconcile. It takes time to rebuild trust, to heal a wounded heart, and to move beyond the hurt. This will happen as people prove their repentance by their deeds. In other words, if they are truly sorry, broken, and repentant, this will be evident by their new actions (2 Corinthians 7:10). But make no mistake about it, God desires for you to forgive others, to reconcile, and to move forward in freedom with Christ. Friend, our God is a God of reconciliation. This was the purpose of His giving Jesus—to reconcile a lost and dying world. This could only happen through the gift of forgiveness He offers to all who will receive. Once you forgive others, then you can begin the journey of reconciliation.

So far we have found out that forgiveness is not forgetting; nor is it automatic reconciliation. Lastly, forgiveness is not for the other person; it's for you.

> **Forgiveness is not for the other person.**

Remember Isaiah 43:25 where God says, *"I am He who blots out your transgressions, for my own sake."* God forgave us for His own sake. It was a measure of His love. He loves us so very much that it was for His own sake that He offered forgiveness. You and I stand forgiven today because of who God is, not who we are. In the same way, when we forgive those who hurt us, we forgive them for who God is, not who we are. If you are waiting on others to deserve forgiveness, you will be waiting a long time to forgive them. If you are waiting on others to say they are sorry, you may never hear these words. This is why forgiveness is not for the other person, it is for you. You are causing yourself great pain when you don't forgive. Do you realize that not forgiving someone is a sin? This disobedience to the commands of God causes the unforgiving heart great turmoil. It causes anxiety, bitterness, depression, and hatred. It can act as a deadly cancer eating at the very core of your soul.

> **If you are waiting on others to say they are sorry, you may never hear these words. This is why forgiveness is not for the other person; it is for you.**

We have the privilege of speaking at marriage conferences all across the country. After one of our sessions on forgiveness, a woman who was obviously burdened came to us. She explained that she had divorce papers sitting on her desk at home. She said that if something didn't drastically change over the next 24 hours, she was leaving her husband. Her marriage had suffered years of neglect and emptiness. There marriage had flat-lined. There was no connection between them. Years of pain had taken its toll on her and her health. At that moment, she looked at us and said, "Are you telling me that I have to forgive my husband for all the things he has done wrong and failed to do right?" Jena reached over and tenderly held her hand. "Yes, sweetheart, you do. You may never hear the words *I am sorry*. You may never hear the words *Will you forgive me*. You certainly didn't deserve this, yet in the midst of it all, you must still forgive." As we concluded, the woman's husband joined us, and we witnessed right before our eyes the forgiving power of God. Her husband became broken before us. He confessed to his sin in the marriage. As they sat in the pew and cried, God mended two hearts. A marriage was restored because two people understood that they were to forgive for themselves and not for the other person.

2 Corinthians 10:4–5 says, *"The weapons we fight with are not the weapons of the world. On the contrary, they have divine power to demolish strongholds. We demolish arguments and every pretension that sets itself up against the knowledge of God, and we take captive every thought to make it obedient to Christ."* What thoughts do you need to bring under the authority of Christ? Remember, so much of the battle is played out on the battlefield of the mind.

Authentic Forgiveness - Letting it Go!

So if forgiveness is not forgetting, and it is not automatic reconciliation, and it is not for the other person but for you, then what is authentic forgiveness, and how do you get there? It starts with the awareness that every one of us stands in need of forgiveness. So many times, we look at other people

> We can honestly say that marriages will change when couples take their eyes of judgment off of their spouses and turn them on themselves.

instead of looking at ourselves. It is so easy to see their faults, their sin, and their shortcomings. We can honestly say that marriages will change when couples take their eyes of judgment off of their spouses and turn them on themselves. This is why the Word of God commands us to do some self-reflection (Matthew 7:3; 2 Corinthians 13:5; Galatians 6:1). It is here that we see the depravity of our souls. It is here that we must be motivated to bring our sin and confess it before a Holy God. Have you ever had someone come to you and say, "Well, if I hurt your feelings, I'm sorry." What is that? That is a lack of owning your stuff apology! We are not talking about glazing it over and minimizing the behavior with an "if I" apology; we are talking about authentic forgiveness. We are talking about confession.

The Greek word for confess is *homologeo*, which means to declare, acknowledge, agree with, profess. Confession of our sins is professing and agreeing with God about our sinful behavior. It is the first step toward forgiveness. We must do this first with God and then with those against whom we have sinned (James 5:16).

So how do you know if someone is just making a blanket apology or if he is truly owning his stuff with the desire to experience authentic forgiveness? This can be very difficult for couples to walk through because most of the time the trust level is very low and the pain is very real. The Word of God reminds us that we cannot judge the motives of another person's heart. We also have to be very careful how we judge others because this is the same way we will be judged. But in the midst of the uncertainty and confusion, there are some indicators of authentic forgiveness. Very simply, true confession will always be partnered with repentance. Repentance (from the Greek word *metanoia*) means to have a change of mind which results in a change in the direction of your will. You recognize you are in the wrong place, headed in the wrong direction. You wake up and agree with God about the choices which led to your sin. Moved by your own helplessness to fix this, you are crushed in your soul to repent of your sins and change. Isn't this the story of the prodigal son in Luke 16? Verse 17 says, "*...when he came to his senses...*" Verse 18 says, "*I will set out and go back to my father and say to him: Father, I have sinned against heaven and against you.*" True confession and repentance always involves returning to our Heavenly Father. It also involves the person against whom we have sinned. Did you see it in the verse?—"*I have sinned against heaven and you.*"

True confession and repentance also results in a changed life. Countless couples have told us, and we have said it too:

"Their words mean nothing to me anymore. I've heard it all before, but things just stay the same." Why is this? Perhaps it is because we are not truly repentant. There is a difference between worldly sorrow and godly sorrow, and 2 Corinthians 7:10 reminds us, *"Godly sorrow brings repentance that leads to salvation and leaves no regret, but worldly sorrow brings death."* It is godly sorrow that causes change in a person's life. Godly sorrow means you agree with God and you see your sin the way He sees it. It causes grief, mourning, and heaviness of your heart until it is dealt with, repented of, and forgiven. This is what it means to be crushed in your soul. In Psalm 51:17 David writes, *"The sacrifices of God are a broken spirit; a broken and contrite heart."* The word contrite literally means to be crushed like powder. This is so powerful because when our spirits are defiant and we are hard-hearted and unwilling to agree with God, sin and suffering continue. But when our spirits are broken, becoming tender and pliable (crushed like powder), the Holy Spirit blows in and washes away our sin.

> **Godly sorrow means you agree with God and you see your sin the way He sees it.**

Worldly sorrow, on the other hand, is experienced when one is simply sorry he got caught. Worldly sorrow involves self-justification and making excuses for your behavior. It is the opposite of repentance because it does not involve true confession, true repentance, and true transformation. It is disobedience to God's Word and it causes emotional and spiritual death. Couples who choose worldly sorrow over godly sorrow live in a vicious cycle of inauthentic forgiveness. Without godly sorrow which leads to true confession and repentance, it is likely they will experience the same issues again and again in their marriage. So many couples have told us they just can't seem to move past the same old stuff. They keep dealing with the same issues over and over again. They say they are sorry, they ask for forgiveness, but

> **Worldly sorrow involves self-justification and making excuses for your behavior.**

nothing ever really changes. The fact is they are very unhappy in their marriages and feel "stuck". The more this occurs and the same sins are repeated, the more untrusting a couple becomes. For true forgiveness to occur, we must ask for the cleansing power of God in our lives. We must ask God to break us, to shape us, and to show us ourselves and our sinfulness so that we truly experience godly sorrow. Then as the psalmist begged in Psalm 51:10, we will pray, *"Create in me a pure heart, O God, and renew a steadfast spirit within me."*

The Choices of an Authentic Forgiver

With confession, repentance, and godly sorrow as our backdrop, let's look at the first of three critical choices an authentic forgiver must choose when faced with the opportunity to forgive. God will certainly use situations and circumstances to convict and direct, but He will not force you to do the right thing. Remember, our problem is not that we don't know what to do, but that we are unwilling to do it. You have a free will to act in obedience or disobedience to God, and you will reap the fruit of your choices. Scripture is clear regarding the law of the harvest. You will reap what you sow. In fact, you will reap more than you sow. The Bible says if you sow the wind, you will reap the whirlwind. If you want to reap love, you must sow love. If you want to reap compassion, you must sow compassion. If you want to reap forgiveness, you must sow forgiveness. The choice is yours. We learned in our reconciliation and remarriage that we cannot force each other to do anything. We have to make choices for ourselves and allow God to work in our spouse.

The Hebrew word for forgive is *aphiemi*. It means to send away, to bid going away, or to depart; of a husband divorcing his wife; to send forth, yield up, let go; to disregard and keep no longer. In other words, when sin enters your relationship, to be an authentic forgiver means you will no longer keep hold of the sin that separates you as a couple. You are willing to accept the consequences of the other person's action, and not hold it against him or her.

As we studied the meaning of the word *aphiemi* we found it odd that Strong's study guide referenced "of a husband divorcing his wife." This didn't sound like forgiveness to us, much less a proper application of the word. But as we pondered the intent and application in the meaning, we realized this is exactly what happens when a divorce becomes a reality in a relationship. You bid your spouse to go away, to depart from you, and you end the relationship. Emotionally and physically, you are no longer bound to them! This is exactly what we are to do with sin! We are no longer to be bound to it. We are to depart from it. We are to disregard it and flee from it, avoiding every appearance of evil (1 Thessalonians 5:22; 2 Timothy 2:22). What if, instead of divorcing themselves from each other, a couple decided to divorce themselves from the sin that has taken up residence in their relationship? How would their marriage look then? We believe they would be living and demonstrating authentic forgiveness.

> **What if, instead of divorcing themselves from each other, a couple decided to divorce themselves from the sin that has taken up residence in their relationship?**

Forgive As Christ Forgives

The first demand of an authentic forgiver is to choose to forgive as Christ forgives. In Matthew 6:12–15, Jesus teaches us to pray this way: *"Forgive us our debts, as we also have forgiven our debtors. And lead us not into temptation, but deliver us from the evil one. For if you forgive men when they sin against you, your heavenly Father will also forgive you. But if you do not forgive men their sins, your Father will not forgive your sins."*

Christ is clearly speaking about forgiveness. There is no room for misunderstanding in these verses. Verse 14 makes a definitive statement of what happens when you do not forgive. Christ is saying *How can you accept my forgiveness and not be willing to offer that same forgiveness to those who have sinned against you?* How hypocritical! You are operating your life under a double standard—one standard of how you wish to be treated; the other, of how you treat those who have wronged you. Choosing to forgive as Christ forgives requires a state of brokenness, humility, and selflessness. Christ is sinless, blameless. He walked this world doing no wrong while being wronged Himself (1 Peter 2:22–25). As He hung on the cross, He spoke the words, *"Father, forgive them, for they know not what they do" (Luke 23:34).* Are you thankful today for God's forgiveness that has set you free from the penalty of sin? Or have you, like so many, forgotten what was paid for your freedom? Those who forget the price that was paid for their freedom often sin and abuse the grace of God by continuing to sin. They have a warped view that God will always forgive them. They routinely stomp and peruse upon the grace of God. Paul, in his writings to the church at Rome (Romans 6:1–7), addresses the relationship between sin, forgiveness, and grace. He asked if grace abounded so that sin could abound the more. His answer was absolutely not! The very measure of grace and forgiveness you offer others will be the same measure you receive. This approach to Christ and forgiveness is not authentic; it is a façade. Forgiveness is offered with strings attached, hidden agendas, and impure motives. There is no grace in these façades of forgiveness because you are forgiving on your terms, not God's. We all need to be reminded of the forgiveness that we so freely accept and so quickly forget. It is through this remembrance that we return to God's mercy and grace, giving mercy and grace to others. As you understand the depth of how much you have been loved and forgiven, you will be compelled to love and forgive as Christ forgives (Luke 7:47–50).

Choosing to forgive as Christ forgives is forgiving completely. We must divorce the sin and hold onto it no longer. It is then that authentic forgiveness will become evident in your relationships. What a paradox. We must die to live; we must be buried to be raised; and we must become a slave to be set free. When we make these choices, what we thought was dead becomes alive again. 1 Peter 3:16 says, *"Live as free men, but do not use your freedom as a cover-up for evil; live as servants of God."* God does not want us to use our freedom to continue to sin but to live as He would have us live. Part of that obedience is to forgive as He forgives. Praise God that you stand forgiven and free.

> As you understand the depth of how much you have been loved and forgiven, you will be compelled to love and forgive as Christ forgives.

Leave the Past in the Past

The second demand of authentic forgiveness is that you choose to leave the past in the past. This choice requires great discipline and self-control. Dale's mom speaks of the bury-the-hatchet principle. Many people in relationships live by this principle whereby you say, "Let's just bury the hatchet!" The problem is that some people bury the hatchet with the handle down, and some people bury the hatchet with the handle up. Those who bury it with the handle up can easily go back and pick up the hatchet the next time a conflict arises. They use the past as leverage and a weapon to win the battle. 1 Corinthians 13 reminds us that love does not keep a record of wrongs. It does not exhume the past sin once it has been forgiven. Aren't you glad that Christ does not bring up all your past sins? Aren't you glad He leaves the past in the past? His forgiveness is genuine because He does not keep a record of wrongs (Isaiah 43:25).

We understand that making this choice, especially in the midst of the battle, is not easy. The battle between our Spirit-led faith and our emotionally-driven feelings is very, very real. That's why authentic forgivers decide what they are going to do before they get into the battle. Just like so many other principles you are learning, this one also showed up as we walked through our days of restoration. Remember, the enemy loves to attack our minds. He loves to pile on a flood of accusations and doubts. He is not happy when a Christian couple makes it. He is not happy when real forgiveness happens. He loves to steal, kill, and destroy anything of Christ in your life (John 10:10)—especially the freedom found through forgiveness. This is why he literally delights in keeping you hostage by bringing up the past. You must never forget: Your enemy always deals in the darkness of your past while Christ always deals in the marvelous light of your future (1 Peter 2:9).

> **Your enemy always deals in the darkness of your past while Christ always deals in the marvelous light of your future.**

Here's how we learned this truth of leaving the past in the past. When we walked away from our knee-to-knee session, the one in which we had confessed our wrongs to each other, we were forgiving and forgiven. Yet three weeks later, the enemy attacked my (Jena's) thoughts and mind. When Dale arrived home, I let the bitterness take over. I said, "Dale, I cannot believe you let those people get on a witness stand and say all those hateful things about me! How could you do that?" Dale looked at me and replied, "Jena, I thought you forgave me for that!" I was instantly reminded of this challenge of authentic forgiveness: choose to leave the past in the past. Now, did bringing up the offense mean that I had not forgiven Dale? Did it mean that authentic forgiveness had not occurred in that knee-to-knee counseling session? No! It simply meant that I made the wrong choice that day. We all make wrong choices. We respond in wrong ways and are faced once again with the need to forgive and be forgiven.

When a sin has been forgiven, you must wage war with your mind and choose not to dwell on it or bring it up again.

The Word of God helps us learn how to do this. In 2 Corinthians 10:3–6 we learn: *"For though we live in the world, we do not wage war as the world does. The weapons we fight with are not the weapons of the world. On the contrary, they have divine power to demolish strongholds. We demolish arguments and every pretension that sets itself up against the knowledge of God, and we take captive every thought to make it obedient to Christ. And we will be ready to punish every act of disobedience once your obedience is complete."*

What does this scripture mean? First, it means we must recognize the source of the battle. If we don't know where the war is fought and who the war is against, we won't know what weapons to use. When you are confronted with remembering the past and returning to the conflict, it will help to remember that your spouse is NOT your enemy! Remembering the past and returning to the conflict is more of a spiritual event than anything else. It is either God resurfacing an area in your life to continue His work of holiness in your marriage, or it is the enemy in his relentless pursuit of destruction (Ephesians 6:12). Oh, we know, it feels personal. And this is our first mistake. Second, we must take our thoughts captive under the obedience of Christ. It is intimacy with our Heavenly Father that allows us to wield the right weapons. It is His Word, His character, and taking on His mind (1 Corinthians 2:16) that become our weapons. Then when life attacks, the pressure rises, and the enemy piles on, you will be able to tear down any stronghold, argument, or pretense that the enemy tries to set up in your life and marriage. In other words, if you have more of Jesus Christ in your life and less of you, then what flows forth will be a choice to leave the past in the past. When we learned to authentically forgive in this manner, we made a covenant to never speak again of the sin that we had committed against each other. The only exception to this covenant was for the edification and building up of others (Hebrews 3:13; 1 Thessalonians 5:11). We would only use our journey to help others facing the same issues and struggles that we faced. That's why we have written this book, asking God to use our real-life experiences to provide help and hope for someone else (2 Corinthians 1:3–4).

Take Initiative to Forgive

Authentic forgivers not only choose to forgive as Christ forgives and choose to leave the past in the past; they also choose to forgive before forgiveness is ever needed. This choice is so very critical because conflict is going to happen; people are going to sin against you and let you down; you will be hurt and disappointed. This issue of forgiveness will not simply go away. It is not a matter of if but when the call to forgive will surface. Because these things are going to happen in relationships, authentic forgivers choose today to forgive tomorrow. We read in John 13 that during His last days on earth, Christ demonstrated His decision to forgive before forgiveness was ever needed.

> **It is not a matter of if but when the call to forgive will surface.**

John 13:1 states: *"Jesus knew that the time had come for him to leave this world and go to the Father."* The Scripture says, *"Having loved his own who were in the world, he now showed them the full extent of his love."* Jesus humbled Himself before those He loved. As He washed the disciples' feet, He demonstrated His love not only verbally but also physically. Let's consider for a moment whose feet He washed that night: Judas Iscariot, who was about to betray Him to His death; Peter, who would deny three times that He even knew Jesus; Thomas, who a few days later, would doubt whether Christ had risen. He washed the feet of the other disciples' as well, including His beloved friends who would fall asleep on Him in the garden when He asked them to keep watch. The all-knowing Jesus knew this would happen. So in washing their feet, Jesus was offering forgiveness before it was ever needed. What an awesome display of love and forgiveness. If we will learn to love like Christ, humbling ourselves before each other, our marriages will be different.

Why love like this? John 13 provides the answer, as Jesus asks the disciples if they understand what He has done for them. *"Now that I, your Lord and Teacher, have washed your feet . . . I have set you an example that you should do as I have done for you. . . . Now that you know these things, you will be blessed if you do them" (John 13:14, 15, 17).*

> **If we will learn to love like Christ, humbling ourselves before each other, our marriages will be different.**

Let's face it. We all have a Judas in our lives who has betrayed us. We all have a Simon Peter in our lives who has denied us. We all have a Doubting Thomas in our lives who doubts we have much worth or much to offer. We have Jameses and Johns who will go to sleep on us when we need them most. People will betray you, deny you, reject you, and doubt you. It is not a matter of if but when. For our relationships to prosper and grow, moving beyond the sin and straining toward authenticity and wholeness, we have to follow the example of Christ. We must choose to forgive before forgiveness is needed. Maybe you didn't do anything wrong. You probably feel the person who wronged you should be washing your feet. Remember that Jesus Christ, perfect in every way, got on His knees and became the foot washer.

Forgiveness always starts with you, not someone else. Matthew 5:23–25a states: *"Therefore, if you are offering your gift at the altar and there remember that your brother has something against you, leave your gift there in front of the altar. First go and be reconciled to your brother; then come and offer your gift. Settle matters quickly..."* But Mark 11:25 states: *"And, when you stand praying, if you hold anything against anyone, forgive him, so that your Father in heaven may forgive your sins."*

Do you get the point? If your brother has something against you, go to him and work it out (Matthew 5). If you have something against your brother, go to him and work it out and forgive him (Mark 11). Regardless of who did what, forgiveness always starts with you. Oh how our relationships would change if we would stop punishing each other and started taking seriously this call to forgive! Authentic forgivers don't wait for their spouses to initiate the healing, transforming power of forgiveness; they recognize that forgiveness starts with them. They forgive before forgiveness is needed, becoming emotional foot washers in their marriage. In and of ourselves, we

> **Authentic forgivers don't wait for their spouses to initiate the healing, transforming power of forgiveness. They recognize that forgiveness starts with them.**

have learned that we are not capable. We are weak, sinful, and void of ability. Anything good in us is nothing more than the supernatural power of God living inside of us (John 15:5). The moment we allowed Christ to take the throne of our lives, His power began to transform our minds. It transformed our relationship, and it transformed the way we viewed forgiveness. Yes, forgiveness can be very, very difficult. Some incredibly painful and evil things have happened to people. But praise God, the Word of God combined with the divine power of God gives us everything we need to be successful (2 Timothy 3:16–17; 2 Peter 1:3–10).

  I (Dale) learned the true meaning of forgiveness while on a fishing trip with my grandfather. We used cane poles on most of our fishing trips, but on this special day, my grandfather pulled out a shinny new Zebco 33 reel. He told me all I had to do was bait my hook, push down the black button, take it back to two o'clock then throw my arm toward twelve o'clock and let it fly. I did just what he said. I baited my hook, took my arm back, threw it forward—but the line went nowhere. I just stood there, beating the water right in front of me making a muddy mess of everything. I looked up at him and said, "Papaw, the rod's broken, it doesn't work!" With a huge grin on his face, he replied, "Son, you forgot to do one thing. You forgot to take your finger off the button!" Friend, that is forgiveness. It is taking your finger off of the pain, the wound, the wrongs that you have done and that others have done to you, and releasing them into the hands of Christ. So let's make this personal. Right now there are some things that you have been holding onto. You have such a tight grip on them that they have literally gripped you! Just as I beat the water in front of me making a muddy mess of everything, so it is with your soul. Today can be the first day of freedom for you. You need to do two things: first, come before your loving Heavenly Father and ask Him to forgive you. You need to receive and rest in His forgiveness. Take your wound, your hurt, your bitterness, and your anger and release them into the hands of Christ. Name the person, the event, and the circumstance. Ask God to restore your heart. Ask for the power of complete and total forgiveness.

"Lord Jesus, I now release (name the person or the circumstance below) into your hands. I forgive them, trusting you with my heart. I ask you to remove all bitterness, anger, and resentment I have felt. I pray for freedom for my soul as I bind my heart and mind to yours. I ask that you would cover each and every circumstance and situation with your grace. Restore the joy of my salvation, Lord, as I am fully restored in your grace and mercy. I thank you for the power of complete and total forgiveness, and I choose this day to walk in wholeness and authenticity, fully loved, fully forgiven, fully free because of your finished work on the cross of Calvary."

As we learned, forgiveness always starts with us. Should you go to the person that needs to be forgiven? Do you need to go to the person and ask for forgiveness? Certainly. The Word of God is clear, and the choice is yours. Will you simply be obedient, do the right thing, and trust God for the rest? Remember, you are not responsible for other people's actions or responses; you are only responsible for you.

Sometimes face-to-face forgiveness is not possible. Some of us have been wounded by people who have passed away, moved away, or otherwise can't be contacted. May we suggest you write a letter to the person who wronged you and offer forgiveness. Perhaps you have wronged someone who has passed away, moved away, and you can't find him or her. Then write a letter asking that person to forgive you. Pray a prayer of release and blessing over the person and then destroy the letter. When you do this, you will find the courage and strength to forgive as Christ forgives, to leave the past in the past, and to forgive before forgiveness is needed. As a result, an authentic, Christ-centered relationship begins to grow and flourish into the wholeness and oneness that God originally intended.

MAKING LOVE

"For God so loved the world that he gave his one and only Son, that whoever believes in him shall not perish but have eternal life" (John 3:16).

Love. Too many couples are operating in accordance with the world's definition of love instead of God's.

Agape is the Greek word for Christ-like love. It means unconditional love—love that remains

> **Too many couples are operating in accordance with the world's definition of love instead of God's.**

constant with no strings attached. It involves choosing to love even when your spouse may be unloving or unlovable. It puts the other's interest ahead of your own. Yet many marriages have been damaged by a selfish, it's-all-about-me attitude. It is an attitude that rules and reigns when husbands and wives focus on themselves and their individual needs. Manipulation of the other is almost always the result.

Remember the chapter entitled "Learning to Love"? Scripture clearly calls all believers to ministry, not manipulation. As Christians, we often can share the love of God with others in our world, but within the walls of our own homes, we are extremely self-centered and demanding of love. We don't view our marriages as ministry opportunities. Instead we focus on our own neediness and selfish wants. Seeking wholeness apart from God, we manipulate each other in alarming ways to get our need for love met.

Yet Christ-like, agape, self-less love is the most fulfilling, beautiful part of the marriage relationship. This kind of love involves commitment, determination, and dedication. It is a choice to love someone. God commands love, with clear instruction in 1 Corinthians 13 on how we should love and why we should love. God has given us a clear, concise, and detailed description of agape love as the benchmark for the kind of love husbands and wives should share.

Have you ever tried to fight with somebody who demonstrates agape love to you? You just can't do it! You can try to be mean or harsh or even serious, but when they are showing selfless, agape love to you, you just can't fight with them. If you are allowing the 1 Corinthians 13 traits of love to be manifested in your life, it is extremely unlikely that you will experience unresolved conflict. In order to truly have a fulfilling marriage, we have got to learn to exercise agape love. For if love is the motivation in all you say and do, then love will never fail. God's Word promises that.

Keep in mind the deep-rooted needs of intimacy and importance, combined with the backdrop of experience that comes from our family of origin. All these dynamics, our personal propensity for selfishness, and the fact that no one ever explained any of this to us in the first place—much less taught us how to be husbands and wives—led us many times to act on our most selfish, primitive instincts.

The good news is this: today you can make a conscious decision to become a minister of love in your marriage. Just know that it will not be easy since we have been trained from an early age to be manipulators. Our journey toward authenticity and wholeness was paved with the conscious decision and commitment to apply the calling of ministry in our marriage.

For example, when our daughter Jorja was 18 months old, she loved strawberry milk. It was a nightly ritual at our house for her to have a glass sometime before bed. One evening Jorja asked for her milk, but we didn't have any. As we explained to her that we wouldn't be able to fix her a glass, she looked directly at me (Dale) and began to wink, smile, and show physical affection. Our son Cole looked at Jena and said, "Watch this, Dad's gonna go get her some milk!" Sure enough, I left at 10:30 p.m., drove to the grocery store, and bought the milk and strawberry syrup so Jorja could have her way. She was on a fast track to becoming a master manipulator of her daddy!

Selfishness and a need for personal satisfaction are happening in marriages continually. Manipulation occurs when a husband and wife, while they are full-grown adults, act like children in big people's bodies. We must learn to give the unconditional, agape ministry of love away to our spouses. The problem is we cannot give away what we do not possess. Therefore, we must come to know the love of the "lover of our souls", Jesus Christ, to ever truly understand love in its deepest and fullest form.

> The problem is we cannot give away what we do not possess.

As you study these four characteristics of God's agape love, we pray that you will see areas in your life that need to change. We pray that your idea of love will go from a selfish perspective to a ministry perspective. After all, Christ clearly says that we must decrease so He can increase; if we want to save our lives, we must lose them; and when we are weak, He is strong. Through the guidance of the Holy Spirit, may manipulation and selfishness be revealed and crucified in our relationships so that His love will permeate our homes for His glory and our joy.

Make Love a Priority

In Matthew 22, Jesus is at the height of His ministry and yet the Jewish leaders are questioning His every move. Does your spouse question your every move? Do you question your spouse's every move? Jesus responded with one thing—love. One of the rulers asked Him, "Out of all the commandments given, which is the most important?" That word important is the Greek word *protos*, which is where we get our word priority. And when Jesus was asked what was to be priority in life, He answered love.

Christ made love the priority of His life. Love was the motivation for everything He did and said. Can that be said of you? We are often motivated by a desire to win, to be right, to be heard, and to get our own way when conflict comes. Jesus Christ made love the heart of all that He was. It was priority for Him. Can your spouse say that loving God and loving him or her is a priority for you? Or have children, careers, and life taken priority over love for your spouse?

> **Love was the motivation for everything Jesus did and said. Can that be said of you?**

We know a couple that are fellow sojourners in the Lord. They challenge us, inspire us, pray for us, and hold us accountable. When we first remarried, our challenge from them was to create a "priority time" to love each other through the gift of undivided attention. They challenged us to make time for each other every day to reconnect from our time apart. We thought we had that priority time at night after the children went to bed while we watched *Andy Griffith* together! But reality was that we were not really connecting at all; we were just sitting in the same room watching television. We needed uninterrupted "talk time". Our friends also reminded us of this: God wants us to teach our children what marriage looks like, but if we take the time to reconnect after the children are asleep, what view of a healthy, loving marriage are we giving to our children? Our children are not seeing it at all if they are already in the bed asleep! My (Jena) first thought was that I would be missing out on time spent with them, but the Lord quickly reminded me that time spent making my marriage a priority before them will have long-term effects on their marriages in the future. If they see us making our marriage priority, they too will make their marriages a priority one day.

So now as soon as Dale comes home from work, we tell our children, "It is time for Mom and Dad to have some time together. Please do not interrupt us unless there is a major crisis! Otherwise, we will let you know when we are finished." Then, we sit together in our den and discuss the events of the day. We talk about all that happened during the day, how it made us feel, and what we need from each other for the rest of the evening. This practice not only helps us reconnect for the rest of the evening but it also shows us that we are more important to each other than anything else that might be pressing. It also greatly lessens the stressful demands that we encounter throughout the evening.

Just think for a moment about some typical, trying days in your home. In our home, I (Jena) would be cooking and Dale would walk in. Though I asked how Dale's day was, I was also trying to get Jorja to take her bath, answering questions from Cole about a project, and trying to answer the phone. Somewhere in that confusion, Dale would head to the recliner because he had no desire to compete for my attention. He had had a terrible day, and now the house was crazy too. So he went to escape into the chair. Then I would get mad at him for not helping me. After all, I had worked just as hard, and my day wasn't over until the children were in bed asleep. So I would walk upstairs with a basket of laundry and drop it at his feet. That would make him mad. After all, he had worked all day long to provide for his family. The least we could do would be to give him a little appreciation. By the end of the evening, I would be furious and not speaking to Dale, and Dale would be infuriated for having to fold sheets. He would give me the silent treatment.

Does this describe your house? This conflict would never have occurred if love had been a priority in our home. If I had stopped what I was doing and given Dale my undivided attention, I would have heard about his terrible day, my struggles could have been voiced, and we could have understood how the other was feeling. Then we could have been encouragers for the rest of the evening. I (Jena) might have sympathized with Dale's stressful day and actually WANTED him to head to the recliner and relax,

> **Making your love relationship a priority can make all the difference in the world as you reconnect and then are able to minister to one another.**

ministering love to my husband! And the same goes if the tables were turned and I had had a bad day. Had we taken the time to make our marriage a priority, Dale would have known my plight and have been able to minister to me. You see, making your love relationship a priority can make all the difference in the world as you reconnect and then are able to minister to each other. As a result, agape love would be overflowing in your home, and your children would receive an accurate representation of a God-honoring marriage.

Matthew 22:37–40 says, *"Love the Lord your God with all your heart and with all your soul and with all your mind. This is the first and greatest commandment. And the second is like it: Love your neighbor as yourself. All the Law and the Prophets hang on these two commandments."* May we all determine, with everything within us, to make loving Let us agree to make God and our spouses the priority of our lives. And may it not be expressed in tongue only but also by the way we live.

Commit to Each Other

God also showed His agape love for us by His commitment. We shudder when we think of our society's view of commitment. Many people refuse to commit for fear that they will have to do something they don't want to do or may miss out on something far better. Their lives are characterized

> **In today's society, many people refuse to commit for fear that they will have to do something they don't want to do or may miss out on something far better.**

by an endless supply of maybes. They are committed only to the degree that it benefits them. If it's about helping another but there's nothing in it for them, you can forget it.

People are placed on the child care volunteer list at church, but if the opportunity presents itself to take a trip to the beach, they just don't show up. They give no notice and don't even search for a replacement, leaving the preschool director with a mess on her hands on Sunday morning. People join a Bible Study class that meets at the same time every week, yet they continually miss because other things "come up". However business meetings, school events, or sporting events are commitments they just have to keep. It seems we very easily commit to the things of this world while spiritual things get put on the back burner. Did that one hit a sore spot?

Years ago we leased a car and quickly found that it is easier to get out of a marriage than to get out of an automobile lease! Unbelievable amounts of paperwork and loopholes and various "fine print expenses" kept coming up. Yet to file for divorce in some cases requires little more than signing a few documents and paying a lawyer. Terminating a covenant made before the Creator of the universe is easier than terminating a man-made agreement. Something is majorly wrong with this picture.

Today people make empty promises and do not follow through then wonder why people don't trust anymore. It is because their words have been cheapened with every unkept commitment, and the enemy rejoices as relationships fall apart with each day that passes.

When I (Jena) was a child, I can remember picking one activity that I would participate in for the year. You can bet that if I made a commitment, my parents would see to it that I remained a faithful part of the team or class until the very last day. Why? They were teaching me the value of commitment. They told me that my word was my honor and that if I committed to do something, I was going to do it even if it killed me. That is not the current attitude of our culture. As a matter of fact, we frequently hear people say this about our government leaders: "They say one thing and then do another; while they talk a good game, they never follow through." As Paul says in Romans, "God forbid!"

For some, commitment only has to be adhered to as long as it makes them feel good. As soon as the feelings go, commitment goes right along with it. So if they *feel* love, they conclude that it must *be* love and they remain in the relationship. But if they don't *feel* love, then they conclude there must not *be* love and thus get out of the relationship altogether and begin searching for someone else who makes them *feel* love. Hear this one truth: while feelings are often important indicators of something much deeper, that is all they are good for. They are not to determine our behavior without first evaluating the whys behind them; otherwise, they can lead us away from the truth. Our feelings can swing us in all directions, tossing us to and fro with every wind of circumstance. We must be careful about allowing our feelings to determine our behavior and responses. Properly processing your feelings and walking in truth is critical to marriage.

If we operated based solely on our feelings, we would have a mess on our hands! Think about it: If parents only fed their children when they felt like it, there would be a lot more starving kids in this world. If people went to work only when they felt like it, they probably wouldn't maintain their jobs for very long. And because people stay committed to their marriages only as long as the feelings are there, the divorce rate is soaring.

> **If we operated based solely on our feelings, we would have a mess on our hands!**

The world we live in tells us that when we feel, we act, and when the feelings are gone, we stop the actions. God's love demands the opposite. We are commanded to act like we love each other whether or not we feel like it! And when we do this consistently, the good feelings follow; but the commitment to obeying and trusting God through faith comes first.

The best definition we have ever heard for faith is by James McDonald who said, "Faith is believing the Word of God and acting upon it no matter how I feel, because God promises a good result."

> **"Faith is believing the Word of God and acting upon it no matter how I feel, because God promises a good result."**
> **~James McDonald**

Notice he did not say "because God promises the result I want." God promises the result He deems best for you—what is for your good. What if we would love our spouses with agape love not because they deserve it or because we feel like it but simply because God commands it? What if we would choose to love them not because they are worthy but because He is worthy?

What if Christ had come to this earth and ministered just as He did, but then went to God and said, "Father, these people are good-for-nothings. I try to show them Your ways and they don't listen. They are a bunch of ungrateful people who do not deserve Your love. Therefore, I have decided not to pay the penalty for their sin." Thankfully, that is not what our Savior did. Instead He looked mockery in the face and bore the sin of the world. He remained faithful and committed to the end. We are to do nothing less. And living out agape love means you love your spouse by committing yourself and your love to him or her forever, even when feelings have faded.

When we honor our commitment in marriage just as Jesus honored His commitment before the Father, God will greatly bless and honor it. Some of you have divorced and are single. Perhaps you need to pray about returning to your spouse and seeking God's help in working through your relationship. Some of you have divorced and are now remarried to someone else. Make your commitment to this marriage for a lifetime.

The most loving thing you can do is to restate your commitment to your spouse. Tell him or her that divorce is not an option, and that it will never be used as a threat when conflict occurs. Make your commitment one that is kept and unwavering to the glory and honor of the One who laid before us the perfect example to follow.

Follow Through with Action

The way that agape love is proven true in the life of a believer is when it is backed by action. *"But God demonstrated His love for us in that while we were sinners, He died for us"* (Romans 5:8). Love must also be demonstrated by action in our marriages, not just communicated with our mouths. We all need more than just lip service in our relationships. Yet have you ever made a comment to your spouse like this: "I shouldn't have to prove myself to you"? Well, let us tell you a secret: yes, you do. Jesus Christ spent much of His life proving the full extent of His love. He proved His love for us all the way to a cruel, rugged cross. We, too, must spend our lives proving our love for our Savior through obedience and proving our love for our spouses through demonstration.

We say it like this: When we got married, there was a "trust-o-meter" placed in our relationship. Since then, everything I have done, am currently doing, or will do in the future directly impacts the trust in the relationship. Our actions either demonstrate a love that builds trust or a lack of love that tears it down.

Many of you may have attempted to demonstrate love but have found that it was not received. Perhaps your spouse says that your actions don't say I love you to them. That can be really frustrating if you are trying hard to demonstrate love as best you know how, but to no avail. Author and speaker Gary Chapman has written an incredible book called *The Five Love Languages*. This book is a must-read for learning to love our spouses, children, families, and friends in ways that they best receive and understand love. Dr. Chapman shares that there are five tangible ways that people give and receive love. If you are giving love to another person who does not recognize love in that way, then it is as if you are speaking another language to them.

When Dale and I began to recognize our love languages as well as our children's love languages, we were no longer spinning our wheels. We were actually loving others in a way that they could understand and thus revitalizing our relationships. There was such a newfound energy and excitement in our marriage as we began to demonstrate love to each other in ways that we understood and recognized as love. It was just as incredible to see our children respond because they understood in new ways the depths of their parents' love.

When our daughter Jorja was beginning school, she struggled with separation. She created awful scenes in the school car line as she cried and begged not to have to go to school because she wanted to stay at home. I (Jena) would cry all the way home, begging God to take care of Jorja. Dale offered to take Jorja to school to save me the tears, but he called after the first day crying too! At one point, we were considering paying someone to take our daughter to school! With a broken heart, I began asking God to help our family survive this struggle and to give us discernment about what to do. In His still, small voice, the Spirit of God whispered, "Spend time with Jorja." Well, I was a bit miffed at that statement. After all, I stayed home with the children and they were with me a lot of the time. But as I pondered this more and more, I realized that though Jorja was with me, she rarely got my complete attention. Jorja's way of receiving love was through spending time together.

So the next afternoon when Jorja came home from school, she and I grabbed a quick snack and then went out to the trampoline to work on her spelling together. It only took about 20 minutes, but the next day there were no tears. The next evening at bedtime, I got under the covers with Jorja and read her a book with the flashlight. Again the next morning, there were no tears. Jorja was no longer struggling with separation anxiety because she was experiencing love in a way that she could receive it.

1 John 3:16–18 says, *"This is how we know what love is: Jesus Christ laid down his life for us. And we ought to lay down our lives for our brothers. If anyone has material possessions and sees his brother in need but has no pity on him, how can the love of God be in him? Dear children, let us not love with words or tongue but with actions and in truth."*

We must learn to be demonstrators of our love for each other throughout our marriage. When couples first fall in love, they constantly prove their love with special gifts, words, and time. But as the years go by, the gifts, words, and deeds wane. We must continue to show love to our spouses. When we demonstrate love to each other regularly, our marriages will bear healthy, fulfilling fruit.

Serve Each Other

As we come to the end of our journey together, we cannot stress the importance that servanthood plays in the marriage relationship. It is a beautiful characteristic of agape love that many miss due to this self-absorbed world in which we live. Instead of serving others, many of us are consumed with being served. Yet God shows us a better way.

> **Instead of serving others, many of us are consumed with being served. Yet God shows us a better way.**

The Greek word for servant is *doulos*. It is a word that describes someone who gives his or her self up to another's will; a slave; to be devoted to another as you disregard your own interest. Exodus 21:1–6 provides a clear parallel between servant and master: *"If you buy a Hebrew servant, he is to serve you for six years. But in the seventh year, he shall go free, without paying anything. If he comes alone, he is to go free alone; but if he has a wife when he comes, she is to go with him. If his master gives him a wife and she bears him sons or daughters, the woman and her children shall belong to her master, and only the man shall go free. But if the servant declares, 'I love my master and my wife and children and do not want to go free,' then his master must take him before the judges. He shall take him to the door or the doorpost and pierce his ear with an awl. Then he will be his servant for life" (Exodus 21:1–6).*

This passage of Scripture is rich with truths about love, servanthood, and marriage through the example of a Hebrew servant. After he had served his master for seven years the servant could choose to remain a servant or to go free. Since the master had given the servant his wife and thus his children, if the servant chose to go free, the master could retain the wife and children as they belong to him. What a beautiful, scriptural picture of God's gift to husbands, bestowing upon them the blessings of a wife and children. We need to understand that we do not own our spouses, and as parents we do not own our children. Rather our mates and our children are gifts from God, entrusted to us for the nurture and care they deserve, just as God Himself has nurtured and cared for us. Couples have a great responsibility to honor each other as the true gift and blessing from God that they are.

The turning point of this passage occurs in verse 5: *"But if the servant declares, I love my master and my wife and my children and do not want to go free."* Wow. This slave can go free, but because of love, he remains a slave. For whom is his love and dedication? Is it for the wife and children? Yes, but it starts with love for his master. In fact, it is the love for his master that causes the slave to experience the pain of being marked. The custom was to take the slave to the doorpost and pierce his ear with an awl so that everyone who looked upon him would know that he was a doulos, a servant for his master. Why is this so important for marriages today? Because when a couple is sold out to Christ and their love is grounded by a servant's dedication to Christ and each other, their marriage will have a "marked" difference. In other words, their marriage will be different because Christ has made a difference.

Servanthood in marriage—when husbands and wives put each other before themselves—will mark them as children of God. When others look at your marriage, God desires that they notice a difference in how you live your life, how you treat your spouse, how you show love to each other. Servanthood is a visible characteristic of love when Christ is the catalyst to serve.

> **When others look at your marriage, God desires that they notice a difference in how you live your life, how you treat your spouse, how you show love to each other.**

Though we may think we have a choice to leave our marriages at any time, we do not. We remain and serve our spouses not because they deserve it but because God deserves it. Love, devotion, and servanthood in marriage is not dependent upon your spouse's worthiness but upon Christ's worthiness. Serve your spouse because of your love for your Master and because He commands you to serve.

This is precisely what Christ demonstrated as He loved us all the way to the cross of Calvary. Philippians 2:1–7 provides us with a glimpse of the depth of Christ's love and His servant heart: *"If you have any encouragement from being united with Christ, if any comfort from his love, if any fellowship with the Spirit, if any tenderness and compassion, then make my joy complete by being like-minded, having the same love, being one in spirit and purpose. Do nothing out of selfish ambition or vain conceit, but in humility consider others better than yourselves. Each of you should look not only to your own interests, but also to the interests of others. Your attitude should be the same as that of Christ Jesus: Who, being in very nature God, did not consider equality with God something to be grasped, but made himself nothing, taking the very nature of a servant, being made in human likeness" (Philippians 2:1–7).*

Christ is the epitome of a servant. The passage beckons us all to join Him in His call to love one another with such depth that we would lose ourselves completely for another. We are challenged to do nothing out of selfish ambition or personal gain but to be humble, recognizing that we are in desperate need of God's help to love and serve as we ought.

Our attitude and our minds should align with Christ's as we see His character outlined before us: Christ was fully God yet fully man. He submitted and aligned His will to His Heavenly Father's, not desiring His equality with God to be more important. But rather He emptied Himself of everything, giving up an honorable position in the perfect place of Heaven, and took on the position of a servant, a doulos, to His Heavenly Father.

Yet unlike the servant of Exodus 21, Christ did not get His ear pierced. He was pierced for our transgressions by the nails of a cruel cross. His servant's heart carried Him all the way to Calvary. More than 2,000 years ago, the world was shown what it really means to be a servant: *"And being found in appearance as a man, he humbled himself and became obedient to death—even death on a cross! Therefore God exalted him to the highest place and gave him the name that is above every name, that at the name of Jesus every knee should bow, in heaven and on earth and under the earth, and every tongue confess that Jesus Christ is Lord, to the glory of God the Father" (Philippians 2:8–11).*

Will you begin to demonstrate the four characteristics of authentic love, perfectly exemplified by our Lord and Savior Jesus Christ? The beauty of choice is that you get to make it. You can continue to operate in fleshly ways in your marriage or you can choose to try God's ways of love.

Matthew 20:26–28 says, *"Instead, whoever wants to become great among you must be your servant, and whoever wants to be first must be your slave— just as the Son of Man did not come to be served, but to serve, and to give his life as a ransom for many."* If you want to become great in the eyes of the Lord, you must become a servant. That requires giving of your life for the sake of another.

Colossians 3:22-24 says, *"Slaves, obey your earthly masters in everything; and do it, not only when their eye is on you and to win their favor, but with sincerity of heart and reverence for the Lord. Whatever you do, work at it with all your heart, as working for the Lord, not for men, since you know that you will receive an inheritance from the Lord as a reward. It is the Lord Christ you are serving."* This perfectly describes the attitude of a slave. Could this describe your attitude as you serve your spouse?

For many of us, the task of serving seems daunting and impossible. Some of you have never served; for you this will be a new challenge. Some of you feel as though you do all of the serving and you are exhausted. Still others are somewhere in between. Be confident of this: God sees you and knows your heart. He will provide you with all you need (grace) as you seek to love Him by serving your spouse and others. But He has one requirement for His grace: He gives grace to the humble. Our attitude must be the same as Christ Jesus, as He humbled Himself and became a servant.

A breath of new life came into our marriage when we committed ourselves to receive God's love and then to give that love away. We committed to making each other a priority. We committed to love in spite of faded feelings. We committed to putting love into action. And we committed to becoming servants unto God by serving each other. Authentic agape love requires nothing less than priority, commitment, action, and servanthood. When we attend to all of these in our marriages, we can sing with the psalmist: *"I waited patiently for the Lord; he turned to me and heard my cry. He lifted me out of the slimy pit, out of the mud and mire; he set my feet on a rock and gave me a firm place to stand. He put a new song in my mouth, a hymn of praise to our God. Many will see and fear and put their trust in the Lord" (Psalm 40:1–3).*

Spiritual Wholeness

"May God himself, the God of peace, sanctify you through and through. May your whole spirit, soul and body be kept blameless at the coming of our Lord Jesus Christ. The one who calls you is faithful and He will do it" (1 Thessalonians 5:23-24).

This is the shortest chapter you will read in this book, and it is without question the most important. In our journey toward authenticity and wholeness, we asked ourselves a couple of very specific and deliberate questions such as, *What did we miss the first eight years of our marriage? How did a Christian couple, doing church, end up divorced anyway?* Hopefully, through the previous pages you have learned how divorce can happen to the best of couples. Even though we've learned about building safety in our home, releasing shame and strongholds in our lives, and demonstrating love and forgiveness, there is still more ground to cover. We have to go deeper. We have to look further. We have to keep looking back at what went wrong, what was missing, and ask, *How did this happen?* As we look back over the first eight years of our marriage, it is easy to see that we were neither ready nor equipped for marriage. Did we even know what it meant to have a godly, Christian marriage? Here's the sad part: during our first eight years of marriage, we had no idea that we had even settled for second best. Unknowingly, we had bought into the "American dream" lie from the world, and it showed in our home. As a result, we poured our energies into all the wrong areas. I (Dale) poured my energy into being a good provider, protector, leader, and decision maker. Having a sexual relationship with Jena was sure to connect us intimately, or so I thought. Yet for Jena, the focus was on the emotional and spiritual side of the relationship. This is the case for many marriages today. Husbands think they have a great marriage if they have great sex. Wives consider the marriage great if there is an emotional connection. They want to know the depths of their husband's heart. Men use sex to connect emotionally with their wives while women use their emotions to connect sexually with their husbands. Very rarely do couples connect spiritually, and when they don't, they settle for second best. The result—an incomplete marriage.

With this realization, we began our search for God's idea of a spiritually whole and complete marriage. Again we started by asking the question, *What is the biblical definition of marriage in the first place?* What we knew was that marriage had to be so much more than procreation, materialism, complacency and co-existence. We knew there was something deep within husbands and wives that God wanted to accomplish in marriage. We also knew that marriage should be exciting, even exhilarating, because it is intended to be the ultimate relationship, created by God for deep, life-changing connection. That's why we now understand and believe the biblical purpose of marriage is transformation. We believe that God desires marriage to be the primary relationship where a husband and wife learn to

> **We believe that God desires marriage to be the primary relationship where a husband and wife learn to grow into the image of Christ.**

grow into the image of Christ. After all, if God's desire for us is to become like Christ (Ephesians 1:4; 4:24), then where else would He do his greatest work except in our marriages? This is why, above all other connections a couple makes, God desires for husbands and wives to connect spiritually. He has a plan for this connection. Bottom line: in a spiritually whole marriage, the husband and wife first develop a spiritual connection. This is what was missing in our first eight years of marriage. This is why a Christian couple can "do church" and end up getting divorced. Is this true of your marriage? Are you spiritually connected? Trust us. Even if you don't get divorced, without a spiritual connection you are missing God's best. Your worldly pursuits and your religious activity must never replace your spiritual intimacy as a couple! Unfortunately, countless couples attempt to fix, change, and improve their marriage by fixing, changing, and improving their spouses. This never works. We know from our own experience that the more we as individuals are transformed and become complete in Christ, the more our marriage is transformed and made complete by Christ. Your marriage will only be as complete and spiritually whole as you are spiritually whole.

We found that 1 Thessalonians 5:23–24 holds some amazing truth for our spiritual connections and shows us how to have a spiritually whole marriage. Read again the scripture at the beginning of this chapter, then we are going to pick apart 1 Thessalonians 5:23. To begin, we see that there is one major benefit (peace) and one major purpose (sanctification), but what does that mean?

Peace

First, God desires for peace to be evident in your marriage. Verse 23 calls God "the God of peace". When Christ, the Prince of Peace, came to earth, He came to bring us peace. As sinners, we were enemies of God. But because of Christ, there is now peace between us and God. Jesus is also what brings peace between you and your spouse. He longs for couples to be at peace with each other. When was the last time you described your marriage as one of peace? We live in a world of busyness and selfishness where there is little hope of peace. Yet God desires for us to have peace. In fact, Christ died so that we would have peace. Isaiah 53:5 reminds us that *"he was pierced for our transgressions, he was crushed for our iniquities; the punishment that brought us peace was upon him, and by his wounds we are healed."* In Philippians

4:6, Paul plainly tells us to not worry about anything but to bring it to God and He will give us peace that will keep our minds and hearts set on Him. Isaiah 26:3 says, *"You [God] will keep in perfect peace him whose mind is steadfast, because he trusts in you."* When we lay our worries at His feet and keep our hearts and minds focused on Christ, He promises a peace that we cannot even understand (Proverbs 3:5–6). Peace is a key benefit of being spiritually whole as an individual and as a couple.

Sanctification

So how do you have peace, especially in this crazy, messed up world we live in? It starts by understanding and embracing the fact that God desires for you and your marriage to be sanctified, to be holy. The Greek word for sanctify is *hagiazo*, meaning to consecrate things to God, to separate from profane things, and dedicate to God. There should be a noticeable difference in your life because of the difference Christ has made in you. This difference should show up in your marriage. Perhaps you have forgotten this. Perhaps this is why you don't have any peace in your life or your marriage.

> **There should be a noticeable difference in your life because of the difference Christ has made in you.**

The great news is that all is not lost. God understands, and He passionately pursues you, reminding you of the heights from which you have fallen and pleading with you to return to your First Love (Revelation 2:3-5). You and your marriage are sanctified, set apart, dedicated to God for His good work. So when someone looks at you and your marriage, they should witness something that God has sanctified. Perhaps it's time for you as a couple to dedicate your marriage to God afresh and anew.

Spiritual Wholeness

Like we've said, after our remarriage we reflected on our first eight years of marriage, which ended in divorce. More than anything, we focused on our lack of spiritual connection. We had been deeply involved in various "churchy" things (ministries). Yet as a couple, we experienced very little of what God desires from our spiritual union. We didn't pray together, we didn't read the Scriptures together, nor did we discuss what God was doing in our lives as individuals. We didn't know what each other's favorite verses were, and why. We did not discuss what our passions were for God nor what we felt God was calling us to do with our lives. There were few moments in our first eight years of marriage where we experienced spiritual wholeness. Our guess is the majority of people reading this book have the same testimony. That's why we believe the epidemic of divorce in this country is due to the lack of spiritual wholeness between husbands and wives. Too many couples have settled for second best when it comes to a spiritual relationship with their spouse. The mentality is that praying together over dinner, attending the same Sunday school class, and even serving with great passion within the church somehow constitute having a spiritual marriage. Yes, these things are important, but if a couple is not intimately walking with God as individuals first, and then together, they are not connecting spiritually as God designed. The external appearance of a spiritual partnership is evident, yet the internal reality tells a different story.

> **We believe the epidemic of divorce in this country is due to the lack of spiritual wholeness between husbands and wives.**

The enemy held us hostage to lies that kept us from being connected spiritually. For me (Dale) the lies were, *Don't pray with Jena. What if you pray wrong? Don't talk to her about God's Word. She knows the Bible better than you do anyway. Who do you think you are? Don't you remember that sin you just committed? It's okay not to talk with* her about God. *Your spiritual life is private, just between you and God. You don't need to share it with her!* With lie after lie the enemy sought to steal, kill, and destroy the spiritual element of our marriage. The truth we now fully understand is that God desires for a couple to develop a spiritual relationship long before anything else. It is only when a couple allows the Spirit of God to lead their lives and their marriage that they will experience lifelong love. The truth was, Jena didn't care what my prayers sounded like; she just wanted to pray with me. She didn't care which Scripture passage we read; she just wanted to be in the Word together. And the more I kept her on the outside looking in, keeping the spiritual union at a distance, the more the enemy divided our home. The facts are simple: without a spiritual connection between husband and wife, a couple cannot have a complete marriage. Successful marriages are those where couples read the Word of God together, pray together, go to church together, and walk with God together, communicating and connecting through the leading of the Holy Spirit.

Spirit, Soul, and Body

The depth of spiritual connection between a husband and wife is the source of power behind true intimacy and passion. It sounds so simple yet it is where most couples struggle the most. Here's how Jena and I jump-started our spiritual intimacy.

We began to take small steps to pray together. We would each take a yellow Post-it note and number the note 1, 2, 3. At the top of the note we would write, *How can I pray for you?* and we would ask each other to fill out three prayer requests. When we were back together that night, we had an immediate opportunity to discuss the reason for the three prayer requests and how they had been answered. Instant spiritual intimacy was launched. We then moved to discussing what was each other's favorite verse, passage of Scripture, and Christian song, and why. We became intentional about finding out what each other's passions were for

God and how we could be a source of encouragement in these areas. Once spiritual intimacy began to develop, we found it easier and more fulfilling to connect in other areas as well. We were experiencing emotional intimacy in our souls and physical intimacy in our marriage like never before. It takes determination to build spiritual intimacy in marriage, but it is so worth it because the blessings God desires to bestow upon you and your spouse will truly transform your marriage into the image of God. First Thessalonians 5:23-24 says that we are made up of three parts—spirit, soul, and body. God desires for us to be set apart, holy, experiencing peace in all three areas. It is the way He designed our marriages to experience power and peace. And when we get this right and keep everything in proper order, a realness, authenticity, and wholeness in the marriage occurs. It will become your reality as a Spirit wholeness first happens, and then an openness of heart and soul, so that both husband and wife can be naked and unashamed. Wow! That sounds familiar. It reminds us of the first marriage and of God's design for them. Do you think He has a different plan for you? Or do you believe that the Lord desires that you would walk with HIM, being fully known and being fully loved? That's what we believe. We also believe God knew that as Adam and Eve walked with HIM they would also be empowered to walk together—spirit, soul, and body. As you begin to experience spiritual intimacy in your marriage, the connections—both emotionally and physically—really change. As Jena and I strengthened our spiritual connection, we learned to discuss other matters. We discussed issues pertaining to work and church, friends and family. We talked about how our children were progressing in school, and how they were developing into the people God wants them to be. As our hearts listened and received each other's thoughts, we tapped into our feelings. Our hearts began to receive how we felt. We shared not just sterile, stale thoughts, but emotions and passion. We began to develop true intimacy. God

> It takes determination to build spiritual intimacy in marriage.

also transformed our understanding of physical intimacy. We live in a world that is sex crazed. No wonder couples fall into the trap that physical intimacy is the thing that matters most in a marriage. Don't get us wrong—sex is a vital part of marriage; it's just not the most vital part. In fact, scripture would conclude that it is the least vital. This is why many couples today experience pseudo-intimacy. They settle for second best when God has so much more in store for their marriage. If you want an amazing sex life as a couple, start by having an amazing spiritual life as husband and wife.

A Complete Marriage . . . and all that goes with it!

A complete marriage—spirit, soul, and body—is not something that just happens one day. It requires daily dedication and commitment. Marriages include moments of great exhilaration and ecstasy as well as moments of sheer endurance. The good news is that the plan and path that God has for us can be full of abundance and joy no matter what comes our way. The more we strive to develop a complete marriage, the more we will experience of that for which the God of peace has sanctified us.

God brought us to a crucifixion moment in our lives. We came face to face with our faith, questioning whether we were really willing to trust God and His Word. If we were, then one thing would be required—obedience. We would have to obey God and His commands as individuals. We would have to begin to live with integrity, honesty, purity of heart, and motive. We would have to let God have control. We would have to take our fears and reservations and place them in the hands of Christ. But we first had to repent of the sin that had separated our intimacy. We then remembered the good things about our relationship, times that we cherished, days of joy and happiness. The wonderful memories of our relationship, combined with the brokenness of how far our sin had taken us, made us fall on our faces fully dependent upon God. It is a beautiful thing because when you are flat on your back with no place to look but heavenward, God steps in. As we repented and remembered, we repeated. We put back into practice the things we used to do to nourish and nurture our relationship. We began acting like we loved each other. We started dating each other again. We began serving each other as true ministers. We learned that the little things really do mean a lot. As time carried us from our past and focused us on our future, God showed up in new and amazing ways. How is it possible? Because God is faithful and true to His Word! He is a God of hope. First Thessalonians 5:24 provides this promise: *"The one who calls you is faithful and he will do it."* God revealed Himself in mighty ways as we walked our road toward authenticity. While we may not have known it at the time, the still, small voice of God was calling us. He so desired for us to walk with Him, to hear His voice, and to trust His heart.

God is calling you as well. He is calling you back into a right relationship with Him. He is also calling you to become a safe mate, to minister—not manipulate, to love, and to forgive. He is calling you to let go of your pride and selfish desires, and to lay down the sword of contention, picking up the sword of His Word to protect your home from the advances of the enemy. He is calling you to humility and commitment. He is calling you to obedience. Friend, God has never let us down. He is true to His Word and to His promises. He is faithful to the end, and He will accomplish His will for you as you yield yourself to Him. You have only one response: *Yes Lord! We will trust and obey.* You've heard it said that it takes two—two to make it and two to break it. We would tell you it takes three—two willing partners and Jesus Christ. We pray you will start today on your journey toward a complete marriage, saying yes, Lord, every step of the way.

FRAGRANCE OF CHRIST

"But thanks be to God, who always leads us in triumph in Christ, and manifests through us the sweet aroma of the knowledge of Him in every place. For we are a fragrance of Christ" (2 Corinthians 2:14–15a NASB).

If you have journeyed to the end of this book, you have proven one thing—that you desire to seek wholeness in your relationship with Christ and with your spouse. If you are a child of God, then your ultimate pursuit is holiness, a life set apart for His glory. And your desire for holiness is not for your glory, but for God's alone. As you strive for holiness, you will receive wholeness in Christ. But in order for holiness and wholeness to develop within you, you must learn to embrace the brokenness that is required.

> **If you are a child of God, then your ultimate pursuit is holiness, a life set apart for His glory.**

Many of you understand brokenness. Some truths within this book may have brought you to your knees over the mistakes you have made in your journey with Christ and in your marriage. God wants your broken heart to bring you into deeper fellowship with Him. He wants to continue His refining work in your life. He desires your holiness too, so that you will accurately represent Him in the world.

But let's face it—the thought of embracing brokenness is not very appealing in and of itself. Quite frankly, none of us enjoy or desire brokenness. We would be content and happy to never experience those growing pains. And that is just it. If we never had experienced brokenness, we would be content just as we are to never grow and go with God. It is through the broken times that God draws us unto Himself and continues the good work He began and will be faithful to complete (Philippians 1:6).

When we went through the brokenness of our marriage, neither of us embraced brokenness at all. As a matter of fact, we fought God tooth-and-nail, like a horse fighting his master's bridle. We had no desire to allow our Master to tame us or to bring us into submission to His authority.

Remember our chapter "Let it Go" about having a contrite heart? The word contrite means to crush like powder. When we went through the devastation of our divorce, we were brought to the end of ourselves, literally, with our hearts crushed like powder before God. Our lives were nothing but broken pieces. But God's work was not complete. He restored our marriage with a purpose in mind.

One day after Dale and I reconciled, Dale was riding in the car listening to a CD by Christian artist Clay Crosse. As he worshipped and communed with God, the song "Stained Glass Window" (by Mark Heimermann and Phil Madeira) began to play. Some of the words to the song are:

> *Just beneath the rafters, in a church of stone,*
> *Lay a stained glass window in the attic all alone.*
> *A work of art forgotten, a treasure thrown away.*
> *Taken from the sunlight, it was just a useless frame.*
> *Oh, the things in life we take for granted*
> *Oh, the things of wonder we could know*
> *Oh, I want to be illuminated*
> *Full of Heaven's light, shining through my life*
> *Let the window of my heart reveal Your love.*

With every word of the song, Dale encountered God's calling to full-time ministry. He quickly called me, and together we confirmed God's calling on our lives to minister to marriages and families in what is now called Stained Glass Ministries. Our marriage had been shattered—ruined beyond all repair, we thought. But God picked us up, cleaned us up, and put the broken pieces of our lives back together again. Then as we allowed the light of His Son Jesus Christ to shine through, what a beautiful stained glass marriage He created.

> **God picked us up, cleaned us up, and put the broken pieces of our lives back together again.**

As we embarked on our ministry voyage, the Lord convicted us about our children. We did not want to remarry only to travel and leave them behind. So to encourage them to embrace our ministry instead of resenting it, we called a family meeting and shared God's call for our family. We shared with them that this was not Dale and Jena's ministry, but God's ministry through our family. We helped them understand that they were a part of this, too. Both Cole and Jorja have joined us whole-heartedly in ministry through singing, running our slides, selling products, and sacrificially serving alongside of us. It is the joy of our hearts to see our children loving and serving the body of Christ.

As we began writing this book, our children began to pray diligently for us. One day, Cole told us that he had something he had written to children that he wanted to be included in this book. This is what God inspired our then twelve-year-old son to write:

> Hi,
>
> I am Cole Forehand. My parents are the writers of this book that your parents are reading.
>
> When I was 7 years old, my parents got a divorce. These were some things I did: When I was afraid, I hid behind couches and chairs. When I was angry, I yelled at them.

I even remember tearing up all of my dad's business cards one day. My dad said, "Cole what are you doing?" I said, "Daddy, I am mad at you for divorcing my mommy."

These were some things I felt: sad, mad, scared, and freaked out. I thought it was my fault, but it wasn't. Look, just understand that they love you the same together or apart.

If you don't know God the right way, pray this with me: "Dear God, I don't want to be empty inside anymore. Come into my heart. Amen."

You can e-mail me at my mom and dad's web site if you need a friend.

Cole Forehand

Moms and dads, husbands and wives, God truly does provide hope for hurting families. Our children, Cole and Jorja, were instrumental in helping us come face to face with the reality of divorce and the effect it had on them. The world glamorizes divorce. It paints a distorted picture of what divorce does to family members.

But brokenness can be a wonderful thing when placed in the hands of God. God loves to take broken things and use them for His glory. God used many people in the Bible, just like you, after they were broken. We believe that He does this to leave no room for question or speculation as to who should receive the glory. It is all about His grace and His goodness. If your marriage seems to be shattered, with no hope for repair, there is hope for you in the person of Jesus Christ. He will lift you up, change you from the inside out, then allow you to encourage and help another along life's journey.

Paul understood this well as he penned, *"Praise be to the God and Father of our Lord Jesus Christ, the Father of compassion and the God of all comfort, who comforts us in all our troubles, so that we can comfort those in any trouble with the comfort we ourselves have received from God" (2 Corinthians 1:3–4).* Paul could embrace brokenness because of the hope that he would one day be able to help another who traveled a similar path.

In the book of Joshua we see a journey to brokenness that offers hope for us today. As the book begins, Moses had just died and Joshua had been appointed by God to lead the children of Israel into the land of promise. Joshua believed God and followed Him with all his heart. As the Lord led Joshua to conquer Jericho, Joshua told the people not to take any spoil from the city because it would bring trouble upon them from the Lord. But one person, Achan, chose not to believe these words. Coveting the treasures of Jericho, he took some things, causing the anger of the Lord to burn against all of Israel. (Our sin does affect more people than just us.)

Therefore, as they approached the city of Ai, which means ruin, and attempted to overcome their adversaries, the Lord allowed them to be defeated at a place called Shebarim, which means broken. Joshua 7:5 says, *"The hearts of the people melted and became like water."*

Have you reached the place called broken? Do you feel that your life or marriage is in utter ruin? When our marriage crumbled in defeat, we realized firsthand that our sin as individuals and as a couple had brought us to this very place.

The cities of Ai and Shebarim are located in central Palestine. Do you know what plant grows in Palestine? Myrrh. The significance of this plant is vital. Myrrh was one of the gifts that the wise men brought to baby Jesus (Matthew 2:11), and myrrh was applied to Jesus' body after His death (John 19:39–40). Myrrh is a small shrub that grows in rocks and sand in Palestine. It produces a fragrance when it is injured or broken. As a matter of fact, the more it is broken, the more fragrant it becomes.

> **Through your broken dependence, you become a beautiful fragrance of Jesus Christ.**

Oh, friend, do you see? When Jesus Christ was broken for you and me, He emitted a sweet fragrance for the world to breathe through His unending, never-changing love. Likewise, when we find ourselves broken and ruined, it is then that we should totally depend upon Him. Through your broken dependence, you become a beautiful fragrance of Jesus Christ. *"But thanks be to God, who always leads us in triumph in Christ, and manifests through us the sweet aroma of the knowledge of Him in every place. For we are a fragrance of Christ"* (2 Corinthians 2:14–15a NASB).

God can take the broken pieces of your life, clean them up, and put them back together again. If your marriage seems to be shattered, with no hope for repair, there is hope for you in the person of Jesus Christ. He will lift you up, change you, and put your life together in a new and beautiful way.

So choose your journey's end. Allow God to write your story. Ephesians 2:10 says, *"For we are God's workmanship, created in Christ Jesus to do good works, which God prepared in advance for us to do."* Let God begin His work of holiness in your marriage. As your holiness leads to wholeness, He will unfold His unique plan for you to share your story. There's a lost and dying world that desperately needs to know the hope you've found in Jesus Christ. He's given you a story, so be ready to tell it for His glory.

God is still in the business of working miracles. It may not be changing water into wine, but He is saving marriages, providing hope, and changing lives. And there is no greater miracle than a changed life. May God richly bless you as you strive to know Him more and honor Him with your life and your marriage.

> **There is no greater miracle than a changed life.**

"May our Lord Jesus Christ himself and God our Father, who loved us and by his grace gave us eternal encouragement and good hope, encourage your hearts and strengthen you in every good deed and word" (2 Thessalonians 2:16–17).

APPENDIX

HOW TO BECOME A CHRISTIAN

This section is the most important one in the entire book. Nothing will not compare to what God will do through your life as you surrender to Him. No marriage will ever reach the heights unless both partners are born again. As you read below, follow the five steps to salvation and accept Jesus as your Lord. When you allow Jesus to become the Savior of your soul and the Lord of your life, you will never be the same again. God will transform you into the person He desires for you to be.

Step 1: Recognize That God Loves You

"For God so loved the world that he gave his one and only Son, that whoever believes in him shall not perish but have eternal life" (John 3:16).

Step 2: Recognize That You Have Sinned

"For all have sinned and fall short of the glory of God" (Romans 3:23).

Step 3: Recognize That Sin's Debt Must Be Paid

"For the wages of sin is death, but the gift of God is eternal life in Christ Jesus our Lord" (Romans 6:23).

Step 4: Recognize That Christ Paid for Your Sins

"But God demonstrates his own love for us in this: While we were still sinners, Christ died for us" (Romans 5:8).

Step 5: Pray and Receive Christ Today
"Everyone who calls on the name of the Lord will be saved"
(Romans 10:13).

"For He says, 'In the time of My favor I heard you, and in the day of salvation I helped you.' I tell you, now is the time of God's favor, now is the day of salvation" (2 Corinthians 6:2).

Today, you can receive Jesus as your Lord and Savior. As you agree with the Scriptures above, simply pray this prayer in your heart:

"Dear Jesus, I graciously receive Your forgiveness of my sins and invite You to come into my heart and life right now. I accept the payment of my sins through Your shed blood. I accept You, Jesus, as my Lord and Savior. Please reveal Yourself to me and become real in my life from this moment forward. Thank You for saving me and for giving me eternal life. I love You and commit my life to You. Amen."

What To Do Now

We want to encourage you to do the following three things as a response to your decision.

1. Tell someone. Tell a close friend, your spouse, even tell us. We would love to hear from you.
2. Find a church home that will baptize you and nurture you in your new walk with the Lord.
3. Commit to grow daily in your new Christian life by reading the Bible, praying, and having fellowship with other believers.

This book is accompanied
by an eight-week, DVD-Driven
Bible Study called

*Let's Get Real:
Bringing Authenticity and
Wholeness to Your Marriage*

For more information about Dale and Jena Forehand,
including additional resources/titles available
in book, video, DVD, and CD formats,
or to book an event,
please visit:

www.daleandjena.com

LaVergne, TN USA
10 March 2011
219615LV00001B/76/P